Reading Psychosis

# Reading Psychosis
## Readers, Texts and Psychoanalysis

Evelyne Keitel

*Translated by Anthea Bell*

Basil Blackwell

Copyright © Evelyne Keitel 1989

First published in German as *Psychopathographien*, copyright © Carl Winter Universitätsverlag 1986

English translation first published 1989

Basil Blackwell Ltd
108 Cowley Road, Oxford, OX4 1JF, UK

Basil Blackwell Inc.
432 Park Avenue South, Suite 1503
New York, NY 10016, USA

*British Library Cataloguing in Publication Data*

Keitel, Evelyne, *1951*-
  Reading psychosis: readers, texts and psychoanalysis,
  1. Literature. Special themes: Man. Psychosis. – Critical studies
  I. Title   II. Psychopathographien. *English*
  809'93353

  ISBN 0–631–15729–8
  ISBN 0–631–16496–0 pbk

*Library of Congress Cataloging in Publication Data*

Keitel, Evelyne.
  [Psychopathographien. English]
  Reading psychosis: readers, texts and psychoanalysis/Evelyne Keitel.
    p.   cm.
  Translation of: Psychopathographien.
  Includes bibliographical references and indexes.
  ISBN 0–631–15729–8   ISBN 0–631–16496–0 (pbk.)
  1. Mental illness in literature.   2. Psychology and literature.
  3. Literature. Modern—20th century—History and criticism.
  I. Title.
  PN56.M45K4413 1989.
  809'.93353-dc 19                                    88-28784
                                                         CIP

Typeset in 10 on 12 pt Paladium by Colset Private Limited, Singapore.
Printed in Great Britain by Billing and Sons Ltd, Worcester.

# Contents

# Acknowledgements

I am happy to acknowledge the debts I accumulated while working on this book. Naturally, I alone am responsible for its shortcomings. Many friends and colleagues read parts or all of the manuscript and offered valuable advice and criticisms: Jeanne Clark, Terry Eagleton, Heinz Ickstadt, Murray Krieger, Yvonne Loritz, Luise F. Pusch, Anna Maria Stuby, Lenore C. Terr and Elizabeth Wright. Ernst-Peter Schneck prepared the glossary. Anthea Bell provided an elegant translation; it was a pleasure to work with her. Paul B. Armstrong read several drafts of the book, made detailed comments and asked searching questions that have sharpened my understanding of crucial theoretical points. Wolfgang Stephan encouraged me at every stage of the writing; I am indebted to him in ways I cannot easily enumerate. My particular thanks, however, go to Wolfgang Iser, without whose help and constructive criticisms, which again and again opened up new perspectives on my subject, this book would not have been written.

An invitation to the Rockefeller Foundation's Study and Conference Center in Bellagio, Italy, provided both time and stimulation for revising this book for the English translation.

Earlier versions of parts of this book appeared in *Weiblichkeit oder Feminismus?* Beiträge zur interdisziplinären Frauentagung Konstanz 1983, Claudia Opitz (ed.), Weingarten: Drumlin, 1984, pp. 239–54; and in *Von Shakespeare bis Chomsky*, Arbeiten zur Englischen Philologie an der Freien Universität Berlin, Elfi Bettinger und Thomas Meier-Fohrbeck (eds), Frankfurt etc.: Peter Lang, 1987, pp. 119–36. I thank the editors for permitting their appearance in revised form here.

# 1
# Introduction

## Psychopathological phenomena in contemporary literature

Delusions and horror figures, fear of death and the longing for it, form the subject of a group of prose texts which have been published and read in increasing quantities since about the beginning of the 1970s. Novels such as *Der Hunger nach Wahnsinn*, by Maria Erlenberger; *J'ai tué Emma S.*, by Emma Santos; *Les mots pour le dire*, by Marie Cardinal; and *Mary Barnes, Two Accounts of a Journey through Madness*, by Mary Barnes and Joseph Berke, describe an individual's distress in direct confrontation with psychotic urges, the paralysis and anxiety he or she suffers, as well as the painful process of long-term treatment and the conflicts inherent in therapeutic interventions. In many novels and stories which do not deal exclusively with psychoses and the possibility of treating them, mental illness determines the course of the action. Psychopathology seems to be one of the central themes of contemporary literature. But how is this phenomenon to be conceptually grasped? What is the nature of such literature, the form of its texts, their effect on the reader, their function within the sociocultural context? Is a new literary genre perhaps coming into being, and how might such a genre as 'psychopathography' be defined?

The mere fact that certain texts take psychopathological material as their *theme* is not reason enough to determine them as an independent genre in contemporary literature. For such a grouping to have critical significance, pathographical texts should display more than one common criterion. Conceptual definitions of such texts by virtue of shared stylistic features turn out to be problematical, since considered purely as literary forms they constitute an extremely heterogeneous body of texts. The one striking feature that all these texts have in common, although it takes different forms, is an 'insistence on authenticity'. Authenticity, however, is not a critical category. Authenticity may be approximately defined only by its intention: an account of 'authentic' experience is meant to increase the credibility of what is depicted, and to decrease the reader's scepticism. As early as the English novel of the eighteenth century, a fictitious 'editor' was invented who had to emphasize the claim of literary texts to veracity. If the narrator in such novels was split into editor and author, in the psychopathographic texts of contemporary literature it is the distinction between narrator and protagonist that has been blurred. Both occupy the same position in the text, the author's ego merging with the narrator's, and the author seems to vouch for the authenticity of the experiences described by the testimony of his own person, whose credibility is unquestioningly assumed. No doubts can be cast upon his ability to represent authenticity. As accounts of personal experience, these texts approach the status of documents. The ego is always in the centre, organizing the plot, the textual strategies and the terms of communicating them. What must initially appear to be a great reduction of potential literary forms (the rejection of an omniscient narrator and the consequent curtailment of the possibilities for commentary, or for playing perspectives off against each other) turns out, however, to be one of the conditions for a further characteristic these texts share: they give rise to some very specific kinds of reader-response.

Psychopathographies prescribe reception processes described by Friederike Hassauer as follows: 'Friends give me back the book *J'ai tué Emma S.*; they stop reading after fifteen pages because it is "too much" for them.'[1] Obviously what is communicated to the reader of such texts is not, say, the dynamic forces of unconscious drives (which psychoanalysis designates as the cause of psychopathological phenomena and the delusions resulting from them). Rather, the reader experiences the same ambivalent or negative emotions that accompany psychotic attacks: pleasure as well as oppression, paralysis and anxiety.[2] In extreme cases, the feelings evoked during the reading of such texts can even make the reader stop reading altogether.

The specific way of responding to pathographic texts is induced by the interplay of extremely diverse formal features, strategies and perspectives. They are differently organized in each text, and must thus be separately analysed for each individual case. No formal schema displayed by all psychopathographies exists. However, the effect of pathographic novels is influenced by the subject that these texts have in common, namely the depiction of psychotic experiences. Psychotic personality fragmentation is the experience of being suspended at the verge of non-existence[3] which cannot be communicated in its full range of content and emotion, either in everyday discourse or through psychological and philosophical theories. Psychotic experiences – like those extensions of consciousness analogous to schizophrenia which are artificially induced by LSD or other hallucinogens – can be interpreted as self-confrontation, as the extreme form of an identity crisis which subsequently brings about radical changes in the affected person's perception of himself and the world around him. Such experiences assume a destructive or at least ambivalent character, and are generally felt to be highly charged with anxiety. There is no intersubjectively established knowledge of psychoses. For that very reason, a number of individually and subjectively based phantasies exist, which may be activated and brought into the reading process.

If a novel takes psychotic dissolutions as its subject, it cannot simply call on experiences known to the reader. That very fact has considerable repercussions on both the form of the novel and the reading process that is initiated through the interaction between text and reader. The question central to the psychopathography genre is: how can a literary text overcome certain specific limits of verbalization, while at the same time allowing for a psychotic experience to be communicated?

### Psychoanalytic literary theory, reader-response criticism and emotions in reading

The subject of this study, the incursion of psychopathological phenomena into contemporary literature, might at first seem to call for a straight psychoanalytic interpretation. Sigmund Freud himself tried to apply the methods of dream analysis to literary works; such a procedure would thus be nothing new. Today, there are several different schools within psychoanalytic literary criticism, schools which try to establish a productive reciprocal relationship between the two fields of literary criticism and psychoanalysis. Such a link, however, has so far proved problematic, since conventional psychoanalytic literary criticism investigates the psychogenesis of the text (i.e. the author's unconscious conflicting drives),[4] studies certain readers' reactions through empirical methods (reactions which are determined by the unconscious of the reader in question),[5] or even determines the protagonists' motivations (which entails postulating an unconscious for fictional characters: a very questionable procedure).[6] In all three cases, conclusions about unconscious *human* faculties are imposed upon a *literary* text. Moreover, psychoanalysis is employed as an interpretative model, a system of knowledge organized from on high which is able to churn out interpretations.[7]

Psychoanalytic literary criticism is too strongly influenced by psychoanalysis – in the final resort, only individual personality structures are of interest in both cases. Psychoanalytic concepts and theories are uncritically applied to a different field, that of literary criticism, which leads to some very questionable interpretative practices. Textual strategies, perspectives and schemata – which are of central concern to literary criticism – recede into the background. Hence, psychoanalytic literary criticism is frequently accused of contenting itself with a naive terminology and not having a philosophically well-grounded concept of what constitutes a literary text.[8]

Even before Freud and the beginnings of psychoanalysis, however, attempts were made to correlate the fields of psychopathology and literature. Curiously, these very early efforts – in their different ways, and to a differing extent – still affect the studies of pathographic literature that are made today. However, little thought is usually given to the circumstances in which these studies originated, their specific idea of what literature entails and the intention of their critical pursuit. If we want to assess the relevance and range of these early attempts to link psychopathology with literary criticism adequately, it seems imperative to give a brief outline of the context in which they arose.

The notion of the artist as genius prevalent in the late nineteenth century was concerned with the psychodynamics of creative processes. The catchphrase of 'genius and madness' implies that creativity and mental illness were thought to be causally connected. Artistic productivity, however, is thereby automatically subjected to a negative assessment. Anton Ehrenzweig, in his book *The Hidden Order of Art: a Study in the Psychology of Artistic Imagination* (Berkeley and Los Angeles, 1967), was the first to explain creativity through a psychoanalytic model without falling prey to the old error of equating genius and madness. At the centre of research into creativity, both of the conventional school and of the new one founded by Ehrenzweig, stands the artistically creative human being, or rather his faculties and gifts. The product of his activity, the work of art itself, remains largely outside the field of such studies.

Pathographically orientated literary criticism, too, tries to make psychology fruitful for literary studies; pathographic interpretations derive their analytic tools from research done in clinical psychopathology. Literary texts are taken as the point of departure in pathographically orientated literary criticism, even if only their plots are analysed, but literature should never be reduced to its contents. Moreover, the ultimate interest of this essentially reductionist method again lies in the person of the author. The plots of novels are examined with a view to whether they allow conclusions to be drawn about any pathological deficiencies in the personality profile of the author concerned. Such hypothetical conclusions are then usually backed up by details from the author's life.[9]

A third area of literary research in which psychological and psychopathological concepts are employed is the history of a literary work's motifs and topics. An approach involving the study of motifs might seem particularly appropriate for the subject of this book, the incursion of psychopathology into literature, since such studies work close to the text, and their interest lies in allowing statements about groups of texts with similar topics. However, this method, too, turns out to be problematic. It aims at 'explaining' literary texts, thus depriving them of their often irritating and unsettling character; the conditions in which unusual effects may occur in the reading process are not taken into account. Moreover, in critical approaches which are concerned with the history of motifs and topics the difference between reality and fiction is frequently blurred. Real people cannot, however, be directly and unquestioningly equated with literary characters. A psychotic going through a severe personality fragmentation is trapped in an autistically self-contained world of illusion, and is scarcely open at all to interpersonal communication. If he meets another human being, say a therapist, he may perhaps hope the encounter will have positive repercussions on the symptoms of his illness and his emotional crises, and effect a change for the better. A psychotic in literature, on the other hand, encountered by a reader as the protagonist (or even just a minor character) in a literary text, is very far from being autistically isolated. Indeed, the protagonist's sickness is one of those literary devices which contribute to a network of interconnecting literary strategies. The function of a psychotic within such a literary frame of reference consists principally, in interplay with the other textual strategies, of controlling the reader's reactions to the text.[10]

It is doubtful whether literary texts really do reflect the pathological personality profiles of their authors, as some literary criticism – of the psychoanalytically orientated school as well as of those schools employing earlier approaches to the subject – implicitly claims. It is particularly improbable in the case of psychopathographies. Such texts take psychotic dissolutions as their topic. That means they centre on a subject area with no intersubjectively established reference in the real world. The central problem faced by psychopathographies is that they must overcome the limits of verbalization encountered in such human borderline experiences. There is no established formula for processing psychotic experience in literary discourse. Thus the author of a pathographical text is forced to make innovations of literary form. He can do so, however, only to a limited degree for, as information theory tells us, it is scarcely possible to communicate a new subject area (in this case a psychosis) by means of absolutely unfamiliar, unprecedented formal innovations. If an author is able to convey in literary discourse dimensions of experience not directly accessible to us in real life, then his work must do more than offer a superficial, naive depiction of mental illness. But the need to discover novel ways of communication which will be understood means that the authors of psychopathographies, or at least the authors of those texts which have unusual aesthetic effects, can hardly be psychotics themselves.

The methods and the implicit claims of psychoanalytically orientated literary criticism are problematical. Moreover, the really interesting thing about psychopathographies is their aesthetic effect, which cannot be adequately explained by the psychological approaches discussed above.

The aesthetic response to pathographical texts is characterized by certain ambivalent feelings which surface during the reading process: pleasure as well as a sense of oppression, paralysis and anxiety, those very feelings, in fact, that are called forth during a psychotic attack. But how can the emotional dimension of reading be conceptualized? The emotions described, as evoked by literature, depend on the communicative function of language: emotional attitudes instigated during the reading process are engendered by textual strategies, strategies that are not always identical with those that prestructure the intellectual processing of the text.

Literary critics have always known that feelings influence our reception of art. Aristotle springs immediately to mind in consideration of the emotions involved in reading. He sees the function of tragedy as to arouse pity and terror, thus inducing a cleansing release of those emotions, which, in his time, were felt to be disturbing.[11] Aristotle's *Poetics* is in fact a critique of the Platonic indictment of drama for stirring up passions in an unseemly way, since in Aristotle's view the audience's subjective participation in fictional events has – at least potentially – a positive value.[12]

However, the effect of fiction cannot be founded on a single principle. Aristotle's theory of catharsis is not comprehensive. It does not account for the fact that many texts have an irritant, frustrating or simply stimulating effect; our intellectual interaction with the text plays a crucial role too, one that must not be overlooked. Aristotle reduces the broad spectrum of possible responses to art to catharsis. Thus, his theory cannot provide a convincing explanation of the fascination that proceeds from reading literature. I assume that this fascination arises from the fact that the rational and the irrational both participate in the reception process, that they often come into conflict, that tensions may arise, and consequently erratic and unpredictable responses can occur.

The New Critics were aware of the tensions between intellect and emotion. They even went so far as to claim that certain cognitive processes are instigated by emotions.[13] The emphasis laid on the subjective dimensions of the cognitive process in the writings of the New Critics is significant inasmuch as they drew up the manifesto of axioms to which all the divergent trends in literary theory react to this day – whether positively or negatively. Frank Lentricchia describes the New Critics' concept of literature as follows: 'Another shibboleth of the New Critics – one worth remembering, given recent attempts to portray them as life-denying formalists – was that literature gives a "special kind of knowledge" of nonliterary, nonlinguistic phenomena.'[14] Although the New Critics recognized the importance of the tensions between the rational and the irrational, and there was even a place for non-verbally communicated knowledge in their concept of literature, they were unable to make statements about this numinous phenomenon. They had no theory whereby non-linguistic phenomena could be conceptualized. They did not discuss, draw upon or assimilate theories like phenomenology or psychoanalysis. Therefore, the New Critics had to limit themselves to intrinsic textual analyses on the one hand, and devastating polemics on the other. They constantly spoke out against the use of psychological terms in discussing the reading processes. René Wellek and Austin Warren, in their *Theory of Literature*, tell us:

> The psychology of the reader . . . will always remain outside the object of literary study – the concrete work of art . . . Psychological theories must be theories of effect and may lead in extreme cases to such criteria of the value of poetry as that proposed by A.E. Housman, . . . [who] tells us, one hopes with his tongue in his cheek, that good poetry can be recognized by the thrill down our spine. This is on the same level as eighteenth-century theories which measured the quality of a tragedy by the amount of tears shed by the audience or the movie scout's conception of the quality of a comedy on the basis of the number of laughs he has counted in the audience. Thus anarchy, scepticism, a complete confusion of values is the result of every psychological theory, as it must be unrelated either to the structure or the quality of a poem.[15]

According to Wellek and Warren, even the slightest deviation from the assumptions of the New Criticism would necessarily end in anarchy.

Northrop Frye, an immediate successor of the New Critics, rightly criticized them for their inarticulateness: 'Here criticism is restricted to ritual masonic gestures, to raised eyebrows and cryptic comments and other signs of an understanding too occult for syntax.'[16] Frye pleads for a democratization of literature. In his *Anatomy of Criticism* he attempts to initiate this democratization by proposing a strict system of classification into which all literary and critical phenomena are to be integrated. But even Frye perpetuates one of the New Critics' misconceptions in viewing the mode of existence of the literary work as wholly self-enclosed and inaccessible to language: 'Criticism can talk, and all the arts are dumb.'[17] Consequently, Frye postulates two different kinds of processing reality, one verbal and one pre-verbal: 'Criticism . . . is to art what history is to action and philosophy to wisdom: a verbal imitation of a human productive power which itself does not speak.'[18] This human productive power consists, for Frye, in what C.G. Jung describes as the 'collective unconscious', i.e. a reservoir of symbols and archetypes which is timeless and accessible to all mankind. Frye bases his comprehensive system of literary typology on Jung's psychology. However, that does not make the pre-verbal area in which he situates literature any less cryptic, since Jung's terms and concepts rest on inadequate foundations too.

In his radical rejection of Freud's metapsychology,[19] Jung not only subverts the Freudian theory of sexual drives by taming the threatening and chaotic sexual energies, he also confines himself to that genetic concept of an unconscious which, temporally speaking, originates in a realm preceding ontogenesis, and therefore exists independently of the individual human being. Whereas Freud answers the question of how the unconscious comes into being dualistically – seeing a phylogenetic and an individual conception as being on equal terms, with an unconscious developing in the latter only because of repression – Jung's unconscious is entirely pre-given. According to Jung, every single conscious impulse arises from far-removed unconscious areas. Speech processes are ego functions (and thus reside in the conscious mind); they have nothing in common with the collective unconscious, which is non-verbal and mystical. Freud concedes that some unconscious impulses are indeed akin to the structures of language, and form patterns. Jung's unconscious, however, eludes cognition.[20]

Frye's theory is based on Jung's concept of a collective unconscious,[21] and thus proves unsatisfactory for mapping out both the pre-verbal area which supplies creative energies and the reading process. According to Frye, both author and reader receive impulses from a collective unconscious, impulses that will be the more effective the less they are influenced by the content of the individual unconscious concerned. Frye's model of the individual unconscious is that of a filter: as soon as too much sediment settles on it, it will inevitably muddy the clear, pure current of symbols emerging from the collective unconscious.[22] In this concept of unconscious processes, emotions have the status of smudges.[23]

The manifestos of the New Critics and their successors prove as inadequate as Aristotle's theory of catharsis to describe the role of emotions in reading. Despite Wellek and Warren's fervent dictum that any attempt to construct a theory of effect will necessarily end in anarchy, the object of this book is just that: I want to account for both the rational and the subjective elements in reading. In sketching out my concepts, I draw heavily upon what Wellek and Warren call 'the structure of the poem', that is, on the textual strategies, schemata and divergent perspectives contained in a literary text. Moreover, I make use of phenomenology and psychoanalysis, the very theories that the New Critics neglected to assimilate. My hypothesis is that the fascination that emanates from reading psychopathographic texts arises from the fact that the rational and the irrational both participate in the reading process, that they come into conflict, that tensions arise and, consequently, erratic and unpredictable responses may occur. In order to outline these tensions – without codifying them – I will address the following questions: how can the actual process of reading pathographical texts be conceptualized? To what extent are the reader's responses pre-structured by what he is reading? Are his reactions to reading psychopathographies contained in the text?

Let me first consider the question of reading. For a long time, reading was regarded as an innocent enough and perfectly straightforward activity; thus, it did not seem particularly noteworthy. Only in the past two decades has the reader gradually moved closer to the centre of our critical attention.[24] The very neglect in which the reader as a significant component in communicating with literature used to be held is now exercising almost a vortical effect which leads to intensive critical research. Today, reader-orientated criticism presents itself as a lively and controversial field.[25] It comprises a multitude of different reader constructs.

Describing the various reader constructs is a possible first step towards mapping out this rather complex area. It comprises the contemporary reader (Hans Robert Jauss), the ideal reader (Jonathan Culler), the super-reader (Michael Riffaterre), the informed reader (Stanley Fish), the intended reader (Erwin Wolff), the empirical reader (Norman Holland) and many more.[26] In comparing the philosophical assumptions that guide these heuristic constructs, it soon becomes clear that decisions about the ultimate cognitive aim of the theory in question lurk within all the different models.[27]

Thus, the contemporary reader is that conglomerate of scientific, philosophical and literary knowledge which constitutes the 'horizon of expectations' (*Erwartungshorizont*) against which a text is read. With the help of this construct, a work's history of receptions can be conceived of as a sequence of differing interpretations conditioned by the connections between the changing horizons of expectations and the text concerned.[28] However, as soon as literature is regarded as a grammar-based system analogous to language – as in structuralism – an ideal reader is required, one whose comprehensive reading competence enables him to decode all the conventions and potentials of meaning in the text.[29] The superreader, on the other hand, consists of a 'group of informants',[30] whose function it is (in the sense of deviation stylistics) 'to recognize the specific character of the style'[31] at certain crucial points in the text, i.e. its patterns, its breaks and discontinuities. Study of the superreader aims at the making of statements about poetic language. In his early work, Stanley Fish employs the model of the informed reader, who has the character of a construct (he must have linguistic and literary competence) but also actually exists, and whose reading experiences should therefore lend themselves to empirical examination.[32] For this very reason, the informed reader is too unsystematic an entity to be of value. Consequently, in his later phase Fish finds himself obliged to abandon this concept. Instead, he takes his own reading processes as the norm and preaches subjectivism – he contends that a text can mean anything.[33] The concept of the intended reader is far more stringent: Erwin Wolff defines it as the 'idea of a reader that has [formed] in the author's mind'.[34] In Norman Holland's work, on the other hand, the personality profiles of actual readers, their individual 'identity themes',[35] provide a fixed and rather static framework within which these readers read and interpret.[36] Holland's reader never meets with anyone but himself in dealing with texts.[37]

The individual features of all these reader constructs are determined by their respective philosophical foundations, as well as by the specific cognitive aims of the reader-response theory in question. The fact that emotions play an important part in our interaction with literature is scarcely ever reflected. Moreover, all the reader constructs presented so far are essentially deterministic: either the reader is dominated by the text (as in Culler's and Riffaterre's theories) or he has unlimited power over the text (as in Fish and Holland).[38]

A way out of this dilemma is indicated by Wolfgang Iser's 'implied reader', a concept that brings into view not any specific reader, but reading, the process upon which the dynamic interaction between reader and text relies. For Iser, meaning is neither pre-given nor arbitrary, but is constituted only in the act of reading. One of his basic notions is that a text has two poles, one artistic (created by the author) and the other aesthetic (the 'concretization' accomplished by the reader). Both poles interact with each other.[39] In his model of the reading process, Iser draws on phenomenology, particularly on Roman Ingarden's theories,[40] to sketch out the text's mode of existence, on hermeneutics to conceptualize the way in which the literary strategies contained in the text are decoded, and on Gestalt psychology to outline the interactions between text and reader.

According to Ingarden, a literary work consists of several layers, each comprising a sequence of schemata, positions, perspectives and strategies. His concept of literature is informed by the classicistic notion that the most noble task of art lies in the symbolic representation of an organic whole. The role that Ingarden therefore assigns to the 'schematized aspects' in his model is that of chiming in 'polyphonic harmony'.[41] The concept of polyphonic harmony, in turn, serves him as a criterion for distinguishing between true and false concretizations: the reader has to process the separate strata in a way that makes them merge.

A lively interaction between text and reader is thus hardly possible, and reading remains an activity which is to a large extent dominated by the text.

On the other hand, the literature of the modernists and postmodernists (James Joyce, Virginia Woolf, Samuel Beckett, Thomas Pynchon etc.), upon which Iser's textual theory is based, is characterized by the very fact that any attempt at creating polyphonic harmony is, from the outset, doomed to failure. In his theory of aesthetic response, Iser draws upon Ingarden's model, but emphasizes the blanks, gaps and vacancies within each of the text's several layers. Iser highlights the difficulties in linking the individual schematized aspects into a harmonious whole. Contoured 'places of indeterminacy' instigate and limit a reading process whose first and foremost aim is to build consistency. Through an interplay of 'retensions' and 'protensions' (i.e. the information provided by what the reader has already read, which subsequently gears his expectations as to what might follow), the reader attempts to convert open gestalts into closed ones, a process which the contradictions and negations in the text are constantly trying to undermine. Thus, the structure of the reading process is an essentially dynamic one which cannot be separated from its temporal dimension.

The 'implied reader' is a concept that embraces both the formal structures contained in the text and the reader's acts of concretization. The reader's responses are written into the text; the aesthetic effect of a text results from a decoding of its many layers, each layer having a double aspect: they are verbal structures on the one hand, and on the other the very conditions which allow the text to be affectively and mentally activated.[42] The idea of a 'correct' concretization – such as Ingarden (and later Culler and Riffaterre) have in mind as an ideal – is not present in Iser, but the idea of an adequate one is: Iser by no means leaves the act of consistency-building entirely open (as do Fish and Holland), but conceives of the interaction between text and reader as a process which – within a range of possible and admissible variations – describes certain patterns and movements.

If one classifies the various reader-response theories according to whether they not only acknowledge but also conceptualize the tensions between the emotional and the intellectual elements contained in the reading process, they fall into two diametrically opposite camps. On the one side, we have critics like Holland and Bleich,[43] who entirely deny that there are intellectual components involved in reading. The individual reader's personality profile – an area of research which should be allowed to remain with the psychologists – is of greater interest to these critics than questions relevant to the study of literature, such as analyses of a text's formal structure, or of the function of emotions stimulated by reading literature. The methods applied by Holland and Bleich are just as subjective as the ultimate aim of their studies; they do not stand up to close examination.[44] On the other side, there are the works of Iser and Jauss, which limit themselves mainly to analysing our intellectual inter-action with literary texts. Neither the theory of aesthetic response as developed by Iser, nor Jauss's reception theory, can be accused of moving too far away from the text as the proper object of literary criticism, or of employing subjective methods. However, Iser and Jauss are almost exclu-sively interested in the cognitive processing of a work of art. The fact that emotions play an important part in our interaction with literature is scarcely ever reflected in their work. Thus, Culler's polemic attack against reader-response criticism is – to a certain degree – justified: 'The experi-ences or responses that modern reader-oriented critics invoke are gener-ally cognitive rather than affective: not feeling shivers along the spine, weeping in sympathy, or being transported with awe, but having one's expectations proved false, struggling with an irresolvable ambiguity, or questioning the assumptions on which one had relied.'[45] 'Shivers along the spine' are difficult to conceptualize with the methods developed by the theory of aesthetic response or by reception theory.

Characteristic of the reading processes contained in and instigated by psychopathographic texts, however, are the tensions between intellectual and emotional elements. These tensions are mirrored in the two opposite camps within reader-response criticism: theorizing is exclusively about subjective factors and conducted with subjective methods on one side, and about intellectual factors and conducted with rigorous objectivity on the other. As a result, problems and tensions arise within the profession which are staged in attacks on the philosophical bases of the positions in question.[46] The tensions derive from the subject matter, from the specific nature of the reading process, which consists in ever-changing relations between various modes of perception. The critics' controversies thus reflect and duplicate the interactions between rational and emotional elements in the reading process. Obviously, the structured field of dynamic interactions between the two cannot be analysed with the methods of reader-oriented literary criticism *alone*.

Subjectivity and emotionality, however, should by no means be equated with irrationality. Subjectivity can perfectly well be understood by rigorous and objectifiable methods. Psychoanalysis – the science of the unconscious – has done particularly good service in providing us with objective descriptions of seemingly erratic feelings. In Freud's writings, the categories of the rational and the irrational, the intellectual and the affective, are subjected to a fundamental reassessment, for in all manifes-tations of the unconscious it is the apparently irrational that is the most significant.

Our conscious and our unconscious reactions are always discontinuous; they lack coherence. The unconscious – although containing material which is repressed by the conscious mind – cannot be simply equated with whatever is repressed. The unconscious is not an objective entity, but a battlefield of tensions, of opposing and conflicting drives, which can be perceived only through their effects (i.e. through dreams, slips of the tongue, jokes, unconscious repetition compulsions, symptoms etc.). These effects form patterns which allow certain conclusions to be drawn about the nature of the very conflicts on which they are based. Psychoanalytic methods permit a conceptualization of the radical break between the conscious and the unconscious. Psychoanalysis thus opens up the opportunity to elaborate on the seemingly erratic and apparently irrational elements contained in the reading process and, subsequently, to describe our aesthetic responses to psychopathographic texts.

I contend that if we want to conceptualize reading processes with all the conflicting factors they involve – factors which play not only on our intellect but also on our emotions – we shall have to complement the rigorously objective methods of Iser's theory of aesthetic response with psychoanalysis. That, however, will mean analysing psychopathographies with the aid of a critical method which has never before been applied to this body of texts. If one opens up a radically new perspective on any subject, it will change, perhaps even to such an extent that the terminology previously used to describe it must be rethought and, if necessary, altered. 'Psychopathography' has for some time been regarded as a valid term in literary criticism;[47] it will be retained in this study, since it obviously calls on an accepted critical understanding of the body of texts to be examined. One of the aims of my book, however, is to redefine the concept of 'psychopathography' itself, step by step, in line with the conclusions to be drawn from the individual textual analyses.

### First hypotheses

My study of contemporary literature is centred on the question of how human borderline experiences – which cannot be adequately communicated either in everyday language or by means of psychological and philosophical theorizing – are depicted in psychopathographies and, related to that question, of how the formal structures of certain pathographical texts contain specific reading effects. I will set out from the hypothesis that some of the emotional elements inherent in psychotic phenomena, pleasure as well as paralysis and a sense of oppression, develop while one is reading psychopathographies, and that the feelings experienced in the reading process are instigated and controlled by the formal structure of the text in question. I see this formal structure as an interplay of various textual strategies. The topic – a psychotic personality dissolution – is merely *one part* of these strategies. That means that I shall have to distance myself considerably from the interpretative procedures of pathographical literary criticism. However, analysis of form and content *alone* will not lead to an adequate understanding of the way in which readers respond to psychopathographies, since their response also depends in part on their literary competence. Pathographical novels first appeal to but then undermine and ultimately frustrate the reading habits acquired from consuming contemporary literature, so that a vacuum is created in which the specific effect of psychopathographies can unfold.

On the one hand, psychopathographies react to that part of contemporary literature which takes the linguistic turn of modern philosophy as its topic. Pointing out the difficulty of correlating life and language has almost become a literary convention in twentieth-century modernist and postmodernist writing. Psychopathographies, however, deal with an area of experience which resists linguistic representation. Now, one of the most striking features of pathographical texts is that they are predominantly written in a highly conventional linguistic style which leaves the *capability* of language to represent 'reality' unquestioned. The literary strategies whereby psychotic experience is communicated are not – or, at least, are not all – marked by the unfamiliarity and strangeness of the subject matter; inaccessible material cannot be communicated in an unknown code. Instead, psychopathographies rely for their effect on textual strategies which are in part taken over from their literary context, and on experiences with reading other contemporary texts.

Mediating texts – which primarily consolidate group understanding[48] – are the genre upon which psychopathographies draw for their linguistic style and certain forms of representation.[49] The form, function and effect of mediating texts are thus of significance for any account of the genre of psychopathography. However, as a very new and extremely heterogeneous genre itself, one which has not yet been adequately studied, the genre of mediating texts has so far defied critical conceptualization. In chapter 2, such a conceptualization will be suggested by classifying the mediating texts as a constellation of three groups, each with its own formal features. Each of these three groups of mediating, group-forming texts – the theoretical, the literary and the imitative types – fulfils very distinct functions for its readers. And all three have a stabilizing effect.

In that respect psychopathographies differ fundamentally from mediating texts, to which they are linked in more ways than just by formal criteria; to stress the analogy between the two genres, I divide psychopathographies into three distinct groups. This classification is apt in so far as the literary, the theoretical and the imitative types of psychopathography react in their different ways to the problem of how phenomena which elude communication can be conveyed through discourse, and each finds a different kind of solution. Above all, however, the effect of psychopathographies is anything but stabilizing.

Chapter 3 centres upon textual analyses of two psychopathographies, both to be classified as the literary type: the novels *Der Hunger nach Wahnsinn* by Maria Erlenberger and *The Golden Notebook* by Doris Lessing. Both are of a paradigmatic character; they take a psychosis as their topic, and instigate reading processes which have – to a large extent – an oppressive effect.

The theoretical type of psychopathography, too, encounters certain limitations of discourse: how can the dynamics of what happens in therapeutic treatment be represented and conveyed in theoretical texts?[50] I use Freud's account of the intricacies of his treatment of the Wolf-Man to illustrate and analyse this problem in chapter 4. Freud created a new type of theory in his case histories, and subsequently developed this new form of discourse to such perfection that the case histories of later generations of analysts seem degenerative; they do not really make full use of the literary and theoretical possibilities of the psychoanalytic case history, as I demonstrate in my discussion of Frieda Fromm-Reichmann's theoretical writings.

I chose Fromm-Reichmann's work for my textual analysis – rather than any other out of the vast number of published case histories – because of a remarkable historical coincidence: the patient whose treatment Fromm-Reichmann discusses in her theoretical writings, Hannah Green (a pseudonym), wrote a novel, *I Never Promised You a Rose Garden*, about her therapy. We thus have two accounts of the same psychotherapeutic process from two different perspectives and written in different discourses. The subject itself, the therapeutic treatment, defies verbalization. However, in the novel *I Never Promised You a Rose Garden*, psychotic experiences are not aesthetically communicated but merely described; I therefore regard it as paradigmatic of the imitative type of psychopathography. The imitative type schematically reproduces the form of the literary type of psychopathography, displays no formal innovations of its own and, in turn, cannot give rise to any unusual and interesting reader-response.

The last chapter of textual analysis discusses a curious hybrid form of psychopathography, intermediate between the literary and the theoretical types. Doris Lessing's novel *Briefing for a Descent into Hell* shares characteristics of both these two groups of psychopathographies, and presents some telling complications for the reading process. To overcome the limits of verbalization, *Briefing* employs a theoretical system: R.D. Laing's theories of psychoses (his concept of the 'divided self') are depicted in the novel's formal structures. At the same time, his ideas are aesthetically subverted by the novel's textual strategies and transformed to such an extent that an abstract, theoretical system can become literature.

The final chapter gives first a systematic account of the theoretical conclusions that can be derived from my textual analyses and, following on from that, a theoretical description of the reader-response characteristic of psychopathographies. A certain sense of oppression which is typically induced by reading psychopathographies arises from an interaction of their individual textual structures, their topic (shared by all psychopathographies) and a 'virtual' dimension (virtual because it cannot be fully attributed to the formal structure of the text in question, but is crucially influenced by a reading competence acquired through the reader's acquaintance with modern literature). The reading process of psychopathographies contains a combination of pleasure and 'unpleasure',[51] of forces running counter to each other: impulses of expansive openness and a counter-controlling movement, i.e. factors of expansion and contraction, alternate. These movements and counter-movements form patterns which will always surface so long as the pathographical texts are adequately concretized. It is both telling and interesting that in all psychopathographies, these patterns are structured in a similar way. They seem to be a *typical* component of the response to such texts. In the final chapter, these patterns are conceptualized and interpreted with reference to Ehrenzweig's psychoanalytic theory of creativity. If one agrees with Ehrenzweig's view that creativity and the normal ego functions are defined by a pattern of *rhythmical* oscillations, then psychosis differs in being characterized by an arbitrary, *arhythmical* alternation between phases which may be partly expanding and partly contracting, or both at once. It is exactly such an arhythmical alternation between pleasurable and oppressive reading experiences that occurs in the responses to psychopathographies. In relation to their shared topic – a psychosis – this means that the reader is allowed a *primarily emotional* experience of the basic structure of psychotic phenomena through reading literature.

# 2

# Psychopathographies and contemporary literature: the question of intertextuality

Characteristic of contemporary literature is a division of the literary market into two radically opposite camps. On the one hand, we have modern and postmodern literature; on the other, a fragmentation into all kinds of different 'literatures', each with its specific sociocultural function.

Literary modernism and postmodernism perpetuate the 'linguistic turn' of modern philosophy, i.e. the general awareness of a fundamental linguistic crisis with which our age is afflicted. Not only literature but also philosophy elaborates on the uncertainties of language. Structuralism and poststructuralism both centre around an analysis of this linguistic crisis, focusing on the formal structures of discourse. Here, language is frequently reduced to its basic operation, to binary oppositions and the way in which they are combined and re-combined.

For Ferdinand de Saussure – the founder of structural linguistics – the linguistic sign consists of two separate spheres: the signifier, the linguistic expression of the sign, and the signified, the concept to which the expression refers according to the conventions of a specific language. As de Saussure's intention lies in the construction of a theory of meaning, he finds himself obliged to stress the idea that language has a reference in the outside world. In de Saussure, the signifier, the linguistic sign, is subordinate to the signified, the concept.

However, this idea is referred by the poststructuralists (as represented, for instance, by the psychoanalyst Jacques Lacan and the philosopher Jacques Derrida) to the realm of metaphysics. In Lacan, the signifier precedes the signified. Whereas in de Saussure meaning is the result of the relation between signifier and the signified, in Lacan (and Derrida) meanings arise only from the combination of signifiers. The signified is thus merely an 'effect of the signifiers'.

In de Saussure, the areas of the signified and signifier are separate from one another. In Lacan, on the other hand, a dividing line runs right through the signifiers; it expresses itself as a resistance to any attempt at creating meaning and significance. Knowledge and language come into conflict: the unconscious constantly undermines signification which, in turn, carries traces of a repressed discourse. (On this point Lacan's theory of discourse differs considerably from that of Derrida, who contents himself with repeated analyses of the arbitrary interchangeability of binary oppositions.)

Even before Lacan, Roman Jakobson argued that the paradigmatic and the syntagmatic (i.e. the vertical and the horizontal) relations presented by de Saussure as the fundamental combinatory rules of language not only correspond to the operation of dreams, as conceptualized by Freud (entailing condensation and displacement), but also to the phenomena, familiar in literary criticism, of metaphor and metonymy, i.e. of similarity and contiguity.

Metaphor (*mot-pour-mot*) and metonymy (*mot-à-mot*) are the key concepts in Lacan's theory. They refer to the two linguistic operations whereby both meaning and desire slide along a chain of linguistic utterances. Metaphorical replacement is based on similarity, metonymic displacement on contiguity: an image can be replaced by another which resembles it, or displaced to another that stands in a relation of proximity to it. If a signifier leaps over the dividing line between the signifiers and takes the place of another signifier, the replaced signifier (which has itself replaced another, and so forth) will still be partially present. One of the central motions in Lacan's theory of a linguistically defined unconscious consists of a constant replacement of linguistic signs, i.e. in the shifting of letters: one letter can replace another, one signifier another, one word another. The equivalence between the two terms concerned – the original one and the one replacing it – lies not in their substance but in their function; both can potentially assume the same position within an utterance. The replaced signifier, however, can never be entirely replaced, but rather will always transfer some of its properties to the signifier replacing it.

For the poststructuralists, meaning thus arises not, as for the structuralists, from the relationship between signifier and the signified, but is a quasi-playful byproduct which surfaces only through an endless replacement and displacement of linguistic signs. In Lacan, the signified (the meaning) slides beneath the signifiers. Language thus contains two different discourses: the first serves communication, whereas the second expresses the impulses of an unconscious, metonymically circulating desire.

The metaphorical replacements and metonymic displacements result in an explosion of meaning. Meaning never simply denotes the speaker's intention. Instead, the shifting of linguistic signs engenders new meanings which are stimulated and sustained by the subject's unconscious desire.

What interests the poststructuralists in linguistic processes, however, is not the functioning of ordinary language but its failure, the moment when meaning disintegrates and explodes. The margins of discourse, and the repercussions emanating from a realm beyond discourse, form the subject of their research.

The same linguistic phenomena are also highlighted by modern and postmodern literature (represented by such authors as James Joyce, Samuel Beckett, Vladimir Nabokov, Thomas Pynchon, Robert Coover, Don DeLillo, Angela Carter etc.). It is one of the outstanding characteristics of this camp in contemporary literature that it conveys the linguistic turn of modern philosophy by refusing to represent a reality independent of linguistic articulation. Literary discourse is no longer used as a reliable medium for describing psychological or socioeconomic realities, but assumes a new dimension.[1] It functions as a system of differentiation that lays itself like a grid over the contingent mass of 'reality', sets it in order, draws distinctions, and only thus creates sense and produces meanings.

In twentieth-century literature, language is self-referential: time and again the mechanism upon which the functioning of discourse rests is acutely disturbed, thus directing the reader's attention away from what is represented and focusing it on the way it is presented. Thus, the process of communication becomes more and more problematical. Literary discourse refers above all to itself, to language, whereas sense and meaning seem to be unreliable, fluid and elusive.

### Postmodernism and the literatures of the counter-culture

The current debates about the unreliability of discourse – highlighted by both philosophy and literature – form the intellectual background against which the second literary camp looks all the more remarkable. For in the 1960s and 1970s a literary counter-culture developed, represented by texts such as Robert M. Pirsig's *Zen and the Art of Motorcycle Maintenance*; Rita Mae Brown's *Rubyfruit Jungle*; Ernst Callenbach's *Ecotopia*; Tom Robbins's *Even Cowgirls Get the Blues*; Kate Millet's *Sita*, and so on. The outstanding characteristic of these 'mediating texts' is that, with apparent *naïveté*, they restore to literary discourse that representational function which has become increasingly problematical since the beginning of the twentieth century. Mediating texts employ literary forms which were developed as early as the eighteenth century, and which, against the cultural and literary background of the twentieth century, seem inappropriate, if not obsolete. The use of conventional literary strategies, perspectives and schemata is not, however, mere imitation. In fact, mediating texts, while making use of conventional forms, are developing new strategies of communication between text and reader. The unusual aspect of the mediating texts is their relation to a relatively clearly defined reading public, within which, although this may at first seem paradoxical, they have tremendous effect just because of their conventional strategies of representation.[2]

Any critical analysis of this literary counter-culture which confines itself to studying the forms and topics of individual mediating texts must inevitably lead to the conclusion that they are trivial. For only when the specific interactions between mediating texts and their target group are taken into consideration – their intentionality of being read only by a limited and well-defined number of people – does their innovative aspect come into view. It is solely through their sociocultural function that these literatures can avoid being categorized as schematic literature.

The second striking feature of mediating texts – apart from their highly conventional and schematic literary form – is the fact that they are extremely heterogeneous: generalizing about so diverse a body of texts is difficult, to say the least of it. If individual mediating texts are examined purely with regard to their content matter, they fall into series of texts which could be given labels such as Literature of the New Left, the Women's Movement, the Ecology Movement, the Gay Movement etc. On the one hand, this definition according to shared topics does bring out the relationship between individual texts as well as their thematic orientation towards well-defined subcultural groups; on the other hand, however, it conceals the very formal structures which run straight across the series of texts, and which all the mediating texts have in common.

For within any such series of texts, there are always three textual types. All three are aimed at one particular counter-cultural group whose objective of changing our society determines the content of the series in question. My criterion for distinguishing between the *theoretical*, the *literary* and the *imitative* types of mediating text – as they will be described in the following pages – lies in the reading processes they entail. Of course, the respective effects of the different textual types – to begin with, I will just label them as 'reflection', 'projection' and 'contemplation' – depend upon certain distinctive literary strategies. Each of the three textual types displays formal similarity to the corresponding type in other series of mediating texts. The different attitudes and responses triggered by the three types allow me, in turn, to define their function both within the group to which they relate and within the wider sociocultural context.

If the split within twentieth-century literature can be characterized as an opposition between different literary discourses – modernism and postmodernism articulating a linguistic crisis, whereas the literature of the counter-culture never even questions the representational function of language – then psychopathographies are situated in an intermediate field between the two. They draw upon certain aspects of both forms of literature. Intertextuality is of the utmost importance. The intertextual references are significant because applying familiar literary strategies in pathographical texts renders alien material (a psychosis) more accessible to the reading public. Moreover, intertextual references play a decisive role in our response to reading psychopathographies: a literary competence acquired through our familiarity with contemporary literature is summoned up by the use of familiar literary procedures, but at the same time – because the context is different – this reading competence is subverted and somtimes even negated.

## Form, function and effect of mediating texts: the case of feminist literature

Unlike modern and postmodern literature, mediating texts have so far hardly ever been analysed. Therefore, I find it necessary to precede my study of psychopathographies with an analysis of this genre, with particular attention to those new strategies of communication between text and reader which are at present emerging, and which affect the aesthetic response to contemporary literature in strange ways.

The fascinating thing about mediating texts is that they have clearly definable effects within the social groups in whose context they arise and to which they relate – a most unusual phenomenon, as compared to other kinds of literature. Literary texts manage to adjust certain shortcomings and deficits in the groups with which they are concerned. This interaction between literary texts on the one hand and social groups on the other is closely bound up with the structure of our counter-cultures.

One example of such a strange mutual influence between a social group and a group of texts is provided by the New Women's Movement and the literature written in its context. Feminist literature does not by any means form a homogeneous body of texts: literary texts as diverse as Marilyn French's *The Women's Room*; Lisa Alther's *Other Women*; Kate Millet's *Sita*; Angela Carter's *Nights at the Circus* and Alice Walker's *The Color Purple* belong to the new feminist literature, as do Nancy Friday's *My Mother, Myself* and Colette Dowling's *The Cinderella Complex*. The last two mentioned are texts which – with respect to their intentionality and the way in which they are read – certainly cannot be described as 'literary'. However, all the feminist texts, diverse as they are in form and content, share one feature: every one of them endeavours to convey *authentically female* experience.

Authenticity – in this context – means an insistence upon the veracity and verisimilitude of the suffering depicted in feminist literature. Often it is seen as being inflicted by patriarchy. In feminist texts, authenticity is evoked by negating the conventional distinction between a narrator and a protagonist: both are condensed into the same position in the text, the (female) author's ego merges with the narrating ego, and the author vouches for the authenticity of the experiences described through her own testimony, through her entire being, whose claim to authenticity is never doubted and whose credibility is unquestioningly assumed. Concentration on one representational aspect, i.e. the protagonist, also means that other characters fade into stereotypes, situational contexts cannot take on any significance of their own, time is generally linear, and the narrative is usually stylistically simple and undemanding. Feminist texts implicitly discriminate against modern and postmodern literature's preoccupation with language in that, with apparent *naïveté*, they restore representation and communication to literary discourse.

The one striking feature that all feminist texts have in common, their claim to authenticity, is insufficient for analysing feminist texts, since authenticity, however much it is emphasized, is not a critical category. Authenticity can be approximately defined only by its function, i.e. its intention of initiating specific reading processes: the credibility of the female experiences depicted is to be increased and the (female) reader's scepticism decreased; inadvertently, however, this results in a reduction of aesthetic distance. Aesthetic distance is of importance inasmuch as it allows literature to be perceived and read as *literature*, and not some other form of text (for instance, a textbook, newspaper or political pamphlet).

And, curiously enough, feminist texts are read in compliance with their claim to authenticity. Even competent readers, readers of literary proficiency, approach these texts as if they were factual reports; they consciously ignore their 'literariness'[3] and instead make them the occasion of heated discussions. Such debates have been part of the Women's Movement from the start. By now, discussion groups on feminist literature have become a firmly established part of feminist activities. The structure of all their disputes consists in the fact that a novel will not be discussed as a *literary* text, that is, the debate is not, for instance, about aesthetic forms or those emotional processes involved in reading novels; instead, literature is treated as if it were a mere conglomeration of well-established facts. The discussions are almost exclusively centred on content, not form, and they implicitly aim at the examination of other women's authentic experiences to see whether they may be assimilated to the individual reader's own stock of experience.

The function of these debates cannot be described independently of the structure and objectives of the Women's Movement. The New Women's Movement is marked by its heterogeneity, pluralism and its rapid turnover of a multiplicity of ideas. It is increasingly inclined to split into many semi-autonomous divisions which are only loosely connected with each other and with the Women's Movement at large. The Women's Movement, contrary to, for instance, the Students' Movement of the 1960s (which claimed to be anti-authoritarian, but in fact had a rigid hierarchic structure) has always fervently opposed tendencies towards an internal hierarchy and leader worship.

What the Students' Movement and the Women's Movement do have in common is the fact that they both define themselves by a Utopian idea of progress; as political forces, both aim to bring about a far-reaching structural change in existing society. Unlike the Women's Movement, however, the Students' Movement had a philosophically based, theoretical concept, i.e. that of Marxism, which in turn was subjected to various assimilations and re-formulations by the 'Critical Theory' of the Frankfurt school. This theoretical edifice gave a clear picture of the sociopolitical aims of the Students' Movement. Certain debates within the continuing theoretical discussions also served to mark the individual stages on the way leading to change, i.e. those immediate objectives which had to be reached first in order to effect the desired fundamental change in the structure of society. There was not always agreement on these immediate objectives, but at least the inner coherence of the movement – a coherence based on the group solidarity and group identity of the individual members – was brought about by a theoretically formulated aim, discussion of the immediate objectives as developed in connection with that aim, and the existence of internal hierarchies among the members.

Not so with the Women's Movement. Matters are a good deal more complicated here. Ideas about the ultimate aim of the movement do exist, but they are not, or are only tentatively, formulated theoretically and in writing. There is no such thing as the one comprehensive and generally accepted theory of the Women's Movement.[4] Nor has the movement emerged as a political force on the basis of a uniform philosophical concept; rather, it is founded almost exclusively upon the actual and subjective experiences of individual women.[5] However, concepts and propositions cannot be drawn from everyday experience without being mediated by theoretical reflection. Consequently, there are almost as many opinions about the specific immediate objectives of the movement, those objectives whereby the desired structural change of society is to be initiated, as there are women to debate them. The very question of what is worth fighting for, and where fighting is simply a pointless waste of energy, calls forth apparently endless discussions, often entailing the formation of new sub-groups.

In my opinion, the lack of a theoretical basis for the Women's Movement, and its direct proximity to ever-changing everyday experience, is to be evaluated as a very positive factor indeed. Dogmatic rigidity, as found in the Students' Movement, is almost entirely absent; the most notable characteristic of the Women's Movement is its creative openness. However, if the outstanding features of a political force are an anti-hierarchic structure, lack of theoretical foundations and creative openness, how can group identity be established and new ideas be integrated?

It is this very problem that feminist texts address: the way in which they depict, as models, those concrete, subjective and individual experiences which are the basis for feminist politics compensates for the lack of a comprehensive feminist theory. The 'I' in feminist texts always speaks as part of the Women's Movement, with the implicit assumption that experience can be shared, and that the individual, social and political conflicts described are characteristic of any woman's life, and therefore of the Women's Movement as a whole. Above all, the experiences aesthetically communicated to the reader are of the kind through which she herself, at least potentially, has lived. Therefore, she can activate them while reading. Through identifications and projections, the reader will assimilate the conflicts and experiences on which the text elaborates to her own stock of experience. Such identifications and projections, however, are extremely unstable entities, since they are not intrinsic to any definite formal strategies and perspectives in the text, though they may be stimulated by them; they are almost entirely produced by the reader herself. The function of these identifications and projections is to mobilize her readiness to examine her individual reading experience – which, after all, is not to be justified on the basis of the text *alone* – in the light of the reading experiences of others. The driving factor in group discussion thus consists of identifications and projections which are connected only by association with the actual text, and which therefore have to be interpersonally tested. Through the formulation of interpersonally acceptable readings in group situations, new concepts for and perspectives on desirable immediate objectives for the Women's Movement can be articulated, questioned, rejected or accepted. In the course of such discussions new ideas, which so far may merely have been floating around, are now made susceptible to language and therefore become generally available. This process is potentially endless. As long as the Women's Movement exists, it will always need new feminist texts in which the subjective experiences of individual women are articulated and which, in turn, give rise to group discussions.

This global function of feminist texts, which is both intrinsic to this type of text and quite different from conventional literature, must, however, be further differentiated, for not all feminist texts affect the Women's Movement in exactly the same way. To begin with, I will distinguish between *literary* and *imitative* feminist texts.

It is a characteristic of the literary type of feminist text that it upgrades the current discussions within the Women's Movement by introducing an essentially new factor. Also, it does not take over the formal schemata developed by earlier feminist texts entirely, but rejects that perfection of form which is typical of schematic literature. The novels of Angela Carter, which are both postmodern and feminist, are good examples of literary feminist texts.

The second group of texts, the imitative type, on the other hand, can be defined by the very fact that it reverts to literary schemata and perspectives which other, mostly literary, feminist texts have successfully employed before, and repeats them without any great variation of content or form. Imitative feminist texts – for instance, Marilyn French's *The Women's Room* or Kate Millet's *Sita* – merely reproduce historically determinable but already superseded levels of discussion within the Women's Movement. Interpersonal examination of individual reading experiences in group discussions is superfluous, for in a way imitative feminist texts themselves mirror such a group discussion, in that they merely re-enact a past phase of struggle. However, imitative feminist texts do have a function which is not to be underestimated, for second-generation feminists, or those women who do not take an active part in the Women's Movement, can gain insight into the nature of feminist group procedures through reading novels.

Co-existing with the literary and the imitative feminist texts, there is another type, the theoretical. This is a curious hybrid genre, for these texts aim to establish a theoretical argument: in Nancy Friday's *My Mother, Myself*, for instance, the repercussions the mother-figure has on any woman's life. Theoretical feminist texts initiate reading processes which do not merely instigate reflection (as is usually the case with theoretical texts), but also allow room for individual identifications and projections. Nor do they by any means dispense with the authenticity highlighted in feminist novels: they interpolate a number of 'authentic' stories which are intended to underline the argument in question. As with literary feminist texts, these theoretical feminist texts can give rise to new ideas and perspectives, and often need to be discussed within the movement.

Literary and theoretical feminist texts are subject to a form of historicity which is extremely rare in literature: unlike other literary texts which are indeterminate by nature, open and susceptible to any number of uses, literary and theoretical feminist texts have a definite intentionality. They are clearly designed with an eye to one specific stage of the current struggles within the Women's Movement. However, as soon as the new element they introduce has been discussed, and subsequently either certain objectives of the movement have been partially revised, or the new element has been collectively rejected, the texts' original function is gone; they are now treated as if they were imitative feminist texts. Frequently they deteriorate to serving merely as a reference – for instance, one might then say, 'As in *The Cinderella Complex*'. Sometimes, a brief reference to a text of this kind can engender a feeling of solidarity, though this instance of solidarity is always linked to the actual conversational situation and creates only a brief, transitory sense of identity[6] – as opposed to the protracted and complicated process of reaching a mutual and collective understanding which takes place in the course of first individual reading, and then group discussion of the literary and theoretical types of feminist texts.

Texts written in the context of the Women's Movement address the problem of how – in view of the precarious theoretical foundation of that movement, of its anti-hierarchic structure and openness to new ideas – group identity and solidarity can be established on the one hand, and new elements assimilated on the other. A comparison of the texts belonging to the literary type and those belonging to the theoretical type of feminist texts has shown that both types, despite considerable formal differences, have the same function: they balance the structural deficits of the feminist movement. The other type of feminist texts – that of superseded literary texts, imitative texts and slogans[7] – also addresses this problem, and may be defined by a function shared by all three subgroups: they manage to create mutual understanding and a sense of identity.

### The different effects of the literary, the imitative and the theoretical type of mediating texts

All three different types contained in the genre of mediating texts have one criterion in common: they balance out the structural deficits of countercultural groups. The literary and in part even the theoretical types may at first be irritant; however, during the reading process the reader will not turn his irritation into painful self-analysis, but merely try, by means of projections, to assimilate the divergent experiences depicted in the text to his or her own stock of experience. Such a basically idiosyncratic reading of the text can then, in due course, be tested in group discussions; if the reader has not entirely neutralized the irritant element dominating his or her own reading process by means of phantasies and projections, an intersubjective consensus arising in group discussion will soon disperse any lingering uncertainties. At the same time, articulating various different readings of a literary text makes it possible either to confirm or to modify the politics of the counter-cultural group in question. Its system of norms – which is by definition precariously unstable and open to change – is thereby stabilized (if perhaps only in the short term).

*All* literature is, to a certain degree, destructive. So far, it has proved very problematical to try to distinguish literature from other, non-literary kinds of text by means of inherently 'literary' characteristics or qualities; even 'literariness', the category introduced by the Russian Formalists,[8] can be only functionally, never ontologically, defined. Negativity is one of the few fundamentals to which almost all literary texts can lay claim; the destructive nature of literature can be either thematic, in that the social norms of the society within which a text is written and to which it relates are dismantled (as is the case in particular in the novels of the eighteenth and nineteenth centuries), or it can be of a kind (as in twentieth-century literature) which is to be defined chiefly through the effect of the text: the recipient's habitual patterns of perception and relating to the world are suspended.[9] Mediating texts, however – because of their twofold stabilizing effect (on the individual reading process as well as on a group's system of norms) – break radically free from any latent negativity or destructivity.

Moreover, mediating texts (like the novels of the eighteenth century before them) imitate the processes through which we understand ourselves and our world. In order to create verisimilitude and to make the strange familiar, they quietly exploit our internalized ways of meaning – creation and interpretation. Literary discourse – in mediating texts as well as in eighteenth-century literature – aims at representing verisimilitude. The language used in these texts is far removed from (and suspicious of) the linguistic self-referentiality dominating postmodern literature.

Typical of all mediating texts is their 'happy ending', yet another criterion taken over from the eighteenth-century novel. Where the 'happy ending' of the eighteenth-century novel, which usually took the form of a marriage, meant first and foremost reintegration into the normative social structure of society, in the mediating texts it is more of an additional assurance to the reader that the problems of conflicting norms he encounters in life as well as literature can actually be solved. What may at first appear a contradiction – the eighteenth-century novel stood for the values and norms of society, while the mediating texts stand for counter-cultural and subcultural norms which aim at subverting society – can be explained by the fact that, in both cases, the institutionalization of norms is at stake.

Thus, the expectation of negotiating and enjoying a stabilizing reading process will become an integral component of the literary competence acquired through reading mediating texts. Subsequently, this literary competence is transferred to other texts with similar formal features. Psychopathographies in particular, which are far from stabilizing and are marked by the destructivity prevalent in all literature, play with this 'horizon of expectations'.[10] It forms the background against which the psychopathographies are read and on which they depend for their specific effect.

# 3

# The literary type of psychopathography

Psychopathographies are about psychotic personality dissolutions, about material which erupts from realms beyond the margins of discourse. A subject area about which there is no intersubjectively established body of knowledge has to be translated into literary language. If the referentiality of a literary text consists of a phenomenon which does not exist outside and independently of its literary representation, but must actually be constituted by it, this has repercussions on both the form and the function of the text in question. At this point, it is important to distinguish between phenomena caused solely by the interaction of text and reader, such as certain feelings involved in reading literature, and phenomena which do exist independently of the reading process, but with which the reader is not familiar from personal experience. The latter type are those addressed in psychopathographies.

Psychosis is a form of mental illness fraught with problems, about which little is known in general. The literary communication of psychotic personality dissolution opens up an opportunity to re-enact the emotional dimensions of such an illness. The experience gained from interacting with a literary text, however, is as much real as fictional, being situated in a curious intermediate area: emotions evoked in reading are real in so far as they are clearly perceptible, but they are also fictional in that they are not caused by anything in the real world, but develop only through processing fictional texts.

The first question I have to tackle in sketching out my model of the way literature instigates emotions is: why do psychoses, as a symptom of mental illness, defy intersubjective communication?

## What are psychotic personality dissolutions?

Metapsychologically – that is, on the basis of psychoanalytic theory[1] – psychotic attacks, together with the violent emotions they release, cannot be comprehensively described, but the structures of the processes involved can. Of the six different concepts of the human psyche developed by Freud in his voluminous work, the topographical and the structural hypotheses[2] are the most suitable for this purpose: they conceptualize the psyche as a spatial entity, and at the same time present it as a constellation of several systems or 'mental localities'. (The individual structural systems – the 'id, ego and super-ego' and the topographical agencies of the 'unconscious, preconscious and conscious' – have divergent functions.) During psychotic states, the 'boundaries' between the mental 'localities' implode, and subsequently the consciousness is flooded with unconscious material which surfaces in the form of primary processes. The primary process characterizes all unconscious activities: it is unstructured and free-floating; psychic energy pulsates in undirected streams. The secondary process, on the other hand, is always directed. It is inherent in all our ego functions, particularly our ability to use language and to structure our environment. Normally, we do not become aware of our unconscious primary processes except in dreams (and even then only in a form greatly distorted by the laws of 'dream-work'[3]), through the mechanisms underlying linguistic jokes and in slips of the tongue. Condensation, displacement and overdetermination – all three are aspects of the dream-work – are functional in so far as they shield the dreamer's consciousness from the perception of unpleasant, conflicting affects and drives. This, however, can be achieved only as long as the individual ego boundaries are relatively intact. If, as in acute psychotic attacks, the ego boundaries dissolve, and their protective function is lost, the ego can no longer undertake its central mediating role between the separate systems contained in the human psyche, since the mental faculties of differentiation and structuring (which are characteristic of the ego functions) regress into a state of non-differentiation, i.e. they fall back to a lower level, one which, in terms of developmental history, has already been surmounted.

This, however, means that psychosis bursts open our habitual and internalized patterns of understanding ourselves and our world, which largely derive from everyday experience. Thus someone confronted with such an experience of inner turmoil will not be able to deal with it adequately. The individual sees himself delivered up helpless to this chaotic state, and feels isolated from his surroundings. If it is hard enough for any adequate intra-psychic reaction to take place, interpersonal communication of the processes which occur during psychotic experience is almost impossible: language is a system of differentiating and interfering signs; undifferentiation cannot be depicted by language if at the same time its communicative functions, such as the conveying and consequently the assimilation of experience, are to be brought into play. Even if the material erupting from the unconscious is, in part, similar to everyday language, those fragments of language that break away from the unconscious (the id) are organized according to the laws of the primary process. Interpersonal communication would first require translation of fragmented, free-floating impulses into some form of regularity, into a linguistic system akin to that of the secondary process. Such a transfer, however, cannot be achieved for the very reason that in psychotic attacks, by definition, the differentiating and structuring ego functions regress to a state of non-differentiation.

Moreover, translating the subjective experiences into language *alone* does not suffice to accomplish satisfactory interpersonal communication: if such phenomena are not to be merely verbally described, but appropriately conveyed, the feelings that surface – ranging from exquisite ambivalence to profound emptiness, paralysis, depersonalization and anxiety – should also be taken into account. This affective dimension originates partly in the dissolution of the ego boundaries, partly in the material breaking out of the individual unconscious. Both are highly subjective entities, and perceptible only to those directly and immediately affected by a psychosis; for the most part, they rule out human discourse and interpersonal communication completely.

Personality dissolutions, therefore, are processes which may be structurally described, but cannot be fully communicated in their subjective and emotional dimensions. However, the very impossibility of communicating such experiences adequately arouses a desire to know more about them. Realms beyond human experience exercise a fascination, a strange mixture of curiosity, anxiety and aversion, on those not afflicted by them: to have the impact of such an experience explained, while one is allowed to remain personally unaffected by it, stimulates the imagination. It offers the 'normal' person the chance of playing with these experiences, and of doing so without having to face any of the dire intrapsychic consequences. This may be *one* reason why the subject of schizophrenic personality dissolutions is at present depicted in many literary texts.

In recent years, moreover, such pathological phenomena have become a focal point of medical research. The ultimate cause of the syndrome is still not clear, and thus therapy is problematical. The diverging hypotheses about the origin of psychosis as a pathological phenomenon range from extreme positions, such as the psychiatrist Thomas Szasz's charge that schizophrenia is not an illness but deceptive labelling,[4] to attempts to explain schizophrenia neurologically as being caused by pathological methylating processes of molecules in the brain. Probably, psychoses are a group of illnesses caused by a multiplicity of factors, which can be understood only if genetic, psychodynamic and social models are all taken into consideration. Medical studies of psychoses aim first and foremost at diagnosis and treatment. The point from which they set out is generally a description of the manifest symptoms. These descriptions, however, do not offer comprehensive information about personality fragmentations; few things are more alike or more drearily monotonous than clinically exact classifications of psychotic manifestations. Apart from that, the communication of the subjective dimension of psychotic phenomena (as encountered by the person affected) is neither intended nor achieved in today's diagnostic manuals.

Psychosis as a pathological phenomenon is a challenge, not only to psychiatry but also to psychoanalysis. Freud was pessimistic about the chances of treating psychotic illness. Nevertheless, in several studies written between 1910 and 1915,[5] he tried to sketch out the theoretical framework for a possible psychoanalytic treatment of psychoses. Two basic concepts provided the criteria for his understanding of this phenomenon: narcissism and libido. In his earlier writings, Freud set out from the premises that there is a fount of libidinal energy which all the different psychic functions can tap. He thought that the amount of libido is *limited* and remains *constant* (an assumption no longer held in modern psychoanalysis). Therefore, he assumed that psychoses necessitate a withdrawal of libidinal energy from the outside world and other people, since it is all needed for narcissistic self-absorption. That, however, means that psychotics cannot build up the transference to the analyst which Freud deemed to be of fundamental importance in psychoanalytic treatment. He coined the term 'narcissistic psychosis', which refers to the self-absorption of psychotics, their engrossment in an autistically isolated phantasy world, their inability to maintain interpersonal relationships, their break with reality, as well as their symptoms of hypochondria, megalomania, hallucinations and delusions.

But some of the analysts who followed Freud partially succeeded in decoding the inner world of mental illness; they even started to develop therapies. Their psychoanalytically orientated theories of therapeutic technique tried to show how an integration of the explosive, unconscious material that threatens the ego-boundaries could or should figure in the psychotherapeutic process.

The point of departure usually chosen by these later analysts is the self-confrontation that occurs during psychoanalytic treatment: both psychosis and the psychoanalytic process estrange the ego from itself, plunge it into identity crises, into great pleasure and great distress. Fragmentation of the ego, its dismemberment, oceanic enlargement and the opportunity of reorganizing it on a new and potentially 'better' level, i.e. one better suited to the individual's needs, are indeed characteristic of psychotic as well as psychoanalytic processes, but in each case they assume a different degree of intensity. During intensive uncovering treatment the self is not shattered to the same violent and destructive extent as in acute psychotic attacks; instead, pangs of anxiety are absorbed by the immense ego-bolstering that occurs in the initial phase of the treatment, and then are further dissipated by the passage of time (psychotic episodes occur explosively, while psychoanalytic therapies unfold over a period of years), by a firmly fixed framework (adherence to the accepted procedures of psychoanalysis, especially to its 'fundamental rule'[6]), and by the psychoanalyst's interpretations, which structure the process and aim to diminish anxiety.

In almost all psychoanalytic writings, the structuring of the therapeutic process initiated by the psychoanalyst's interventions and interpretations occupies the foreground. It is not too difficult to theorize about the structure to be imposed upon the psychoanalytic process, that is to say, about potentially *constricting* factors. The dimension of actual and subjective experience shared between analyst and analysand (the processes of transference and counter-transference) – as opposed to the analyst's interventions – actually represents an *expansive* factor; transference evades and even resists conceptualization both in the treatment of psychoses and in Freud's original form of psychoanalysis.

Obviously, we are here confronted with a problem of discourse similar to that encountered in any attempt to verbalize and convey psychotic experiences: it is the expansive elements, those that break free, which elude communication. However, since in psychoanalytic treatment the expansive elements represent the very realm wherein psychic change is to be initiated and subsequently effected – the intended processes of personality change occur mainly in the dim zone between structured process and affectively charged eventfulness – to conceptualize this dimension is as desirable as it is difficult.

Because of the extreme degree of self-confrontation contained in psychoses (and in the psychotherapy of psychoses), they evade language and communication: apart from the fact that both phenomena are subjective in nature, the emotions involved form a strongly expansive factor. And if verbalization of both the inner world of psychoses and the emotions connected with the experience of undergoing psychotherapy turns out to be difficult, it verges on the impossible to convey both areas simultaneously, either in everyday language or in theoretical discourse. Psychiatric and psychoanalytic research into psychosis has indeed been carried out, but communicating those dimensions of feeling that surface during psychotic phases, or the intricacies of experience entailed in treating the illness, has inevitably faded into the background because the aim of most scientific studies lies elsewhere.

Communicating psychoses is a challenge to the flexibility of discourse.

The prerequiste for depicting the full impact of psychosis and of psychotherapies is translating one mode of thinking into another: unconscious images and impulses – which emerge only in primary process thinking – must be converted into the laws and structures of the secondary process. However, an effective dimension (the emotional world of psychosis and the processes of transference and counter-transference) has to be conveyed simultaneously, and that borders on the impossible. This dilemma of discourse exercises a vortical effect on literature: experimentation with language as a highly differentiated system of interfering signs – which on the surface defy non-differentiation – is as much a characteristic of literary texts as their constant attempts to push into realms beyond the margins of discourse.

### Two paradigmatic psychopathographies: Maria Erlenberger, *Der Hunger nach Wahnsinn* and Doris Lessing, *The Golden Notebook*

Thematically, psychopathographies centre on the depiction of psychoses. Moreover, during the reading process of such literary texts, the emotional dimensions involved in psychotic experiences are conveyed to the reader. The problem addressed by modern and postmodern literature, namely, how to deal with the loss of the representational functions of language, is also of central relevance to psychopathographies: within the psychopathographic genre, this problem is taken up on the thematic level in that these texts are about human borderline situations which defy interpersonal communication. The linguistic problem addressed by psychopathographies is: how can something which is beyond the margins of discourse be communicated in language through a literary text?

This question constitutes the perspective from which I shall analyse the psychopathography genre. Like mediating texts – upon which psychopathographies draw for some of their literary strategies, though not for any stabilizing effect – they are divided into three types of text. With mediating texts, the different ways in which they negotiate and influence the structural deficits of subcultural groups determined the classification of the texts; with psychopathographies, the criterion is the different ways in which individual texts react to the problem of communicating something which lies beyond communication. In psychoanalytically orientated case histories, this problem is dealt with in theoretical discourse; in the literary and imitative type of psychopathography, it is tackled by means of literary discourse. The imitative type of text is degenerative in that human borderline situations are merely described and not transmitted. The literary type of psychopathography, on the other hand, definitely conveys an impression of expansion and openness which can tip over into oppression, and may even cause the reader to stop reading.

The diffuse sense of oppression instigated by reading processes is partly linked to the one theme all psychopathographies have in common: a psychotic personality dissolution. This theme requires the translation of unconscious images and impulses surfacing in the form of primary processes into literary discourse which adheres to the laws of the secondary process.[7] Such a transposition is anything but a 'rejection of verbal communication' (Peter Gorsen):[8] any disintegration of formal linguistic structures would prevent the reader's producing the mental images which form the basis for his or her involvement in the text. Instead, psychopathographies reduce the complexity of psychotic experience to a schema of textual strategies, some of which are transferred from the genre of mediating texts to a new context. Other literary procedures are idiosyncratic to the particular text concerned, and must therefore be examined separately in each psychopathography.

The communicatory situation of all psychopathographies consists, thus, of the topic 'psychosis' and a bundle of textual strategies transposing that topic into literary discourse. The interplay of topic and literary strategies allows the communication, specific to each text, of a phenomenon that resists communication – that aesthetic communication whereby I shall define the psychopathography genre.

Maria Erlenberger's novel *Der Hunger nach Wahnsinn* (Reinbek, 1977) is paradigmatic not only of the entire textual group of psychopathographies but also of that particular sub-group which I call the literary type of psychopathography. The novel is about anorexia nervosa, a mental illness of the schizophrenic type. It describes its protagonist's sojourn in a psychiatric hospital and, in flashbacks, the gradual development of her psychosis. Behind her manifest symptoms – her decision to reduce her intake of food by stages and finally reject it altogether – there lies a painfully achieved self-denial, an attempted suicide by starvation, which leads to a collapse of the circulatory system linked with acute psychotic attacks.

The most remarkable of the idiosyncratic literary procedures of Erlenberger's novel is the interlocking of two different levels of representation. Interpolated into descriptions of the psychiatric context, the hospital routine, the behaviour of the other patients and the present emotional state of the narrator, are flashbacks to the various stages of her slide into mental illness. The two time levels are intertwined in such a way that the chronology of events is constantly interrupted. The two levels of representation are kept separate by the consistent use of a different verbal tense in each: the present for the psychiatric context, the past for the retrospective flashbacks. The distinction between the two tenses indicates a clear conception of space and time in the first-person narrator, who is presented as schizophrenic; the entire internal world of the text is unfolded through this narrative perspective. The condensation of the poles of author, narrator and protagonist into a single position in the text is – as opposed to the idiosyncratic and rather striking use of tenses – one of the factors borrowed from the genre of mediating texts.

The literary strategies employed in *Der Hunger nach Wahnsinn* may make it possible to describe something which evades verbalization, but they do not by any means present it mimetically: in this novel, the author has refrained from dismantling formal linguistic structures, as she has also refrained from presenting the dissolution of a clear conception of space and time in the narrator's mind. Both, however, are integral components of psychotic personality dissolution.[9]

The interlocking of two different levels of representation results in the opposition, characteristic of first-person novels, between a narrating ego and an experiencing ego, but Erlenberger's text immediately breaks with one convention of the (traditional) first-person novel, namely the idea that it should be possible to discern a 'narrating ego which now, looking back, presents itself as more experienced, mature and purged' (Franz Stanzel).[10] The retrospectively handled realm of the experiencing ego merges with a psychic reality which remains unchanged, and in which the narrating ego is still involved; the description of the inner world of psychosis is not confined to the retrospective flashbacks, but constantly reverberates in the narrative frame. Both levels of representation, the retrospective level and the narrative frame, merely offer different perspectives on the narrating ego's unmediated and continuing affliction with psychopathology. Thematically, this is manifested in the way the narrator's imagination circles constantly around her symptoms. Her initial obsession with a painful rejection of food, far from being overcome on the level of the narrative frame, is turned into its opposite, expressing itself as an anxiety-ridden insistence on eating:

> I long for food, whatever it's like. I am so greedy, I'm so oppressed, I feel it, it cuts me off, I am in such trouble, there's no room for me, I'm in such straits, I can't free myself, I flail around me in my mind. I rise and fall, I live and I want to die, I have fallen into the waterfall of my brain and I must give in to it. (p. 59)[11]

The two levels of representation mirror one another; the narrating ego is neither more mature nor mentally healthier than the experiencing ego.

The plot of the novel does not make an impact on the narrator's frame of mind: no changes occur either in the story or in the protagonist. Corresponding to the narrator's acute psychotic attack and her subsequent admission to hospital, described at the beginning of the book on the retrospective level, there is a further psychotic attack to which the narrative frame leads at the end. Thus the ending does not just remain open: rather, it becomes obvious that the novel is about stasis, immobility and rigidity. The parallel levels of representation have no temporal dimension, but always remain the same; no changes (for better or for worse) take place, and therefore no ending is possible.

The tensions vibrating between the two levels of representation induce different illusions of a time continuum, a phenomenon which strongly influences the reader's responses to the novel.[12] The retrospective level is marked by the exclusive and consistent use of the historic past, a tense well suited to comprehensive accounts from a standpoint far-removed in time. During the reading process, the reader has to produce mental images which, in turn, he needs in order to build consistency[13] out of the contingent information offered by the novel. The reader's centre of orientation is of crucial importance for the quality and the amount of mental images produced, and his centre of orientation is undoubtedly situated in the narrative frame. Thus the flashback episodes appear, as one reads, to be already in the past. Moreover, the fragments of plot contained in the retrospective level are narrated in chronological order. (Even though the novel begins with the provisional climax of the narrator's mental illness, i.e. her committal to a psychiatric clinic, this climax is followed by detailed accounts of the separate stages of the illness itself.) An illusion of events occurring in a time continuum is evoked by the construction of a chronology, while the serial arrangement of the individual fragments of narration is instrumental in establishing the illusion of an inner causality akin to that of a plot. Therefore, the psychopathology depicted must strike the reader as extremely determinate, and the development of the protagonist's sickness must be conceived as a compelling necessity.

The illusion of an unavoidable determinacy is enhanced by the narrator's explicit insistence on authenticity, a device which, as I have already described,[14] is characteristic of mediating texts and is obviously taken over from that genre. In *Der Hunger nach Wahnsinn*, as in most of the mediating texts, authenticity, evoked by information given on the back cover the book, is brought into play as a strategy of verification:

> Maria Erlenberger presents a confession of great and general significance. Her book, written in a psychiatric hospital, is not one of those investigations into human distress (meritorious as they are). . . . 'I will risk my life for myself' – the author reaches this state of recovered identity only behind closed doors. Thus the hospital becomes the 'ex-centric place', the stop on the way to 'existence', as Jacques Lacan has put it.

On the second level of representation – that of the psychiatric context – the chronology of the narrative is shattered: episodes from the psychiatric context and the emotional state of the narrating ego are described in the present tense. Thus the very possibility of plot development is undermined; the narrating ego is no farther on than the experiencing ego at any point in her discourse, but is constantly being overtaken by her life. There is no narrative distance between the describing agency and what is described. Events arise and fade away; they are never brought to any satisfactory conclusion, but coincide with the time required to depict them: the narrated time collapses into the narrating time. The contingent and additive arrangement of fragments interchangeable in terms of their content, the resorting again and again to the same scraps of plot, suggest that the narrative can be repeated to infinity; the concrete shape of the text takes on a dimension of irritating randomness. It appears to be nothing but one among many possible such shapes.

This form of representation prevents the reader from producing mental images of a certain kind. Instead of the idea of a time sequence, the illusion of a continuum of perception is contained in reading the narrative frame. The reader cannot bring his own projections to bear. Moreover, his attempts to build consistency – which constitute one of his most important activities during processing a literary text – become potentially an irritant.

The two parallel levels of representation, the repeated return to the same fragmentary events, the randomness of the formal structures of the text and the open ending suggest that the narrated events are rampant and explosive. The potentially limitless variability and the arbitrariness of the one central theme, the protagonist's psychopathology, are documented in ever more facets and aspects. Even the digressions into the chronologically arranged flashback episodes provide no pause, and do not dam the narrative flow, but only establish a highly unstable frame of reference for the events described on the level of the narrative frame (the psychiatric context). The instability of the frame of reference results from the fact that the retrospective level centres around an endless and obsessive repetition of the same events. What at first might seem informative will soon cease to be so, and the repetitions – which are of great linguistic but only slight semantic variability – finally appear entirely devoid of meaning. They no longer present an attempt to convey the nature of anorexia, but merely give the impression of something obsessive, repetitive and unreal, which in turn is an integral component of psychotic processes.

Thus, on the one hand, writing can be interpreted as a defensive operation: defence mechanisms take on the obsessively repetitive form of primary processes. Moreover, the attempt at articulation in this novel is not the condition for working something through, but represents the endeavours of an ego threatened by disintegration to save itself as it founders. On the other hand, however, the device of different, interlocking levels of representation, the interchangeability of the individual narrative fragments, and the constant return to what stays always the same cause all linguistic and narrative structures to collapse. The narrative flow seems to expand endlessly. In this, it corresponds to those expanding and rampant emotional dimensions which are integral components of psychotic processes and potentially defy verbalization.

The textual strategies contained in Erlenberger's novel are marked by a specific ambivalence. They are both rejection and communication of what cannot be said: rejection in that they are highly structured, and thus are not by any means a mimetic depiction of psychotic phenomena; communication in that integral components of psychotic phenomena are conveyed by the very nature of this structure.

Apart from the idiosyncratic treatment of time in *Der Hunger nach Wahnsinn*, this psychopathography adopts all those representational criteria I set out above, in sketching out the function of mediating texts, as characteristic of this genre: characters other than the protagonist who are introduced into the narrative, in particular the hospital staff, her fellow patients and her friends and relatives, are never described as rounded individuals, but are reduced to stereotypes, to mere props; they are not able to influence the course of events. The situational context, the psychiatric hospital, is present all the time, but acquires no intrinsic value for the plot. The language, too, is conspicuously simple; the text consists of syntactically correct sentences, only the imagery is notable.

The narrating ego's imagination circulates obsessively and repetitively around the rejection or intake of food, that is, around those areas within which the symptoms of anorexia manifest themselves:

> Eating and I, drinking and I, these have always been landmarks in my life. I have made them my life itself. Blown them up into a huge bunch of flowers. Roses, sunflowers, stinging nettles, lady's smock [Translator's note: *Schaumgummikraut*, 'lady's smock', if literally translated would mean 'foam rubber plant'.] My bunch of flowers, all in order, arranged to precise rules, co-ordinated with each other. Spellbound by this task, I almost forgot life in the process. (p. 50)

The symptoms are described in their capacity of setting 'landmarks', and thus endowing the contingent temporal flow of life with a structure that seems to invest it with meaning. The structuring element of the symptoms becomes the *tertium comparationis* for the ensuing metaphorical language borrowed from nature mysticism: various flowers are 'blown . . . up into a huge bunch . . . all in order, arranged to precise rules'. An alienating optical impression is thus given of an object which in itself is very commonplace, food. According to Harald Weinrich's definition, this is a 'bold metaphor':

> not because it diverges so far from ordinary observations, but because it diverges so little. It does not transport us to an entirely different sphere, but takes us just one small step farther . . . it depends on the span of the image whether we notice the contradiction and feel the metaphor to be bold. Where the span of the image is large, the contradiction usually remains unnoticed. A small span, on the other hand, forces us to notice the contradiction, and gives the metaphor the character of boldness.[15]

The span of the image in the metaphor quoted above is a *small* one, for the reason that human nourishment, like flowers, may be classified as something natural, something encountered and used every day. The innate contradiction necessary to all metaphors, not consciously perceived but taken in subliminally and without preceding intellectual value judgement, is the fact that flowers are indeed natural products but are not at all edible. Who would think roses, sunflowers, stinging nettles or lady's smock appetizing?

The optically striking nature of the metaphor translates the ambivalence inherent in every psychotic symptom into discourse: the fascination that arises from the possibility of structuring the contingent flow of time is overshadowed by a sense of disgust evoked by the idea of having to eat flowers, particularly flowers whose colloquial names contain a reference to industrial products ('foam rubber plant'). A commonplace thing like food is represented, by the specific way it is expressed in language, as both fascinating and inedible, whereas in a synaesthesia like 'I relish the taste of my dreams' (p. 75) the two sensory areas are exchanged again: the sense of taste is transferred to a primarily optical process (dreaming).

Sensations of physical dissociation are integral parts of psychotic phenomena. Jacques Lacan has coined the term 'phantasm of the dismembered body' to characterize them or, more precisely, to describe the fact that analysands often dream of dismembered parts of their bodies during phases of their analysis in which they regress far back into realms of undifferentiation. Gisela Pankow defines the phantasm of the dismembered body as a characteristic symptom of all psychotics, that is, not just those who, like Erlenberger's protagonist, display the symptoms of anorexia nervosa. Pankow contends that psychotics are incapable of 'restoring the wholeness of life when a part of the body is missing'[16] and of 'allotting their proper and specific functions to the individual parts of the body'.[17] In Erlenberger's novel the phantasm of the dismembered body surfaces in the protagonist's phantasies:

> My weakness lying down became so overwhelming that I stared at
> the corner between ceiling and wall with fixed eyes which appeared
> to me one single eye – like a part of the body in itself. I could not and
> would not move this giant eye. I had no way to make it move. My
> body lay relaxed and yet rigid. It was as if it were separate from me. I
> was empty, I had a hollow ring to me, I was unending. An empty
> head which was my whole body, and a hole in it which was this eye,
> staring at a space that was also my hollow head. (p. 24)

The optical dimension, which plays a central part in both metaphors
discussed above, is here personified and condensed into a single giant eye.
However, what is highlighted is no longer the exchange between different
sensory areas; instead, the narrator's sensitivity is undifferentiated, compressed and encompasses all her physical feeling. Eyes always carry an
unusually high effective charge:[18] they regulate perception, our way of
understanding and interpreting our world and, according to Lacan, access
to the symbolic order of language. They are close to the brain, not only
because of their location in the body; they are cerebral, they control and
structure the secondary process. It is this very function which fails in
the passage quoted: any movement of the eye – which must precede
perception – appears impossible.

The spontaneous, subliminal connotation of this image is a sense of
paralysis, while paralysis, in turn, is an integral component of anxiety
processes. In combination with the expansive openness prestructured by
the textual strategies, these and similar passages in the text build up a
communicational situation between text and reader which may propel the
reader into a sense of oppression. Emotional reactions to the communicatory situation – that is, to the interaction of topic, textual strategies and
metaphors – occur within the tensions between what is actually said and
what is only subliminally understood, but is present by the very fact of its
omission. Thus the recipient reacts emotionally to something not explicitly verbalized in the text.

Anxiety itself *is* verbalized in the text:

> So I go on my ghost train, the fairground ghost train in my brain.
> I've been on it so often. It is my life. I know the horrors that spring
> out at you, always at the same spot. Here – there – a ghost – some-
> thing white – a blow from behind – a shrill siren – filaments
> dancing before my eyes – Death with his scythe darts past my
> heart – and there is the fear again – it is the same familiar old ghost
> train I know in this world. (pp. 25f)

Suddenness as a way of perceiving something unexpected, accidental, out
of context, entirely new, entirely alien, outside the planning of anticipa-

tion, is one of the forms in which anxiety surfaces in psychotic episodes. In the passage quoted, suddenness is suggestively evoked in the metaphor of the fairground ghost train. The reader knows what fairground ghost trains are, and what it is like to go on them. Therefore, he can assimilate the semantic field in question – the impact of suddenness – by associating it with certain emotions with which he must be familiar. At the same time, however, the emotional dimension of anxiety inherent in psychotic personality dissolutions is transferred to a semantic field alien to it. Thus, the horrors can be *explained* through recognition of the incidents that usually do occur in fairground ghost trains. Here anxiety is translated into literary discourse only in a weakened, unsatisfactory form.

Anxiety phenomena are verbalized in many passages of the text in a similar way, that is to say, transferred to other areas: 'Fasting was hard. Time was so long. I was dried up and so empty. The fear of eating after all was great. I must not do it, whatever happened, or my system would collapse and my life fall into utter disorder. Sense disintegrated, as if exploding, and struck me hard on the soul' (p. 55). The fascination emanating from the rejection of food obviously consists in the opportunity of structuring time through this psychotic symptom. Simultaneously, however, there is an underlying dimension of *angst*. According to Sören Kierkegaard,[19] *angst* threatens existence and is undirected, a feeling that overwhelms the individual concerned, although no actual cause for it can be discerned; fear, on the other hand, is directed, related to a definite object which is perceived as frightening. In the passage quoted, what is expressed is not so much *angst* (*angst* being an integral component of psychotic processes) as fear. *Angst* is transferred: modified, named and thus also personified as the fear of breaking a self-imposed rule of fasting – that is, as fear of something definite. Erlenberger's text translates fear into literary discourse, rather than that dimension of *angst* which is inherent in every psychosis and fundamentally threatens existence. Fear of something familiar and well known is more amenable to description than *angst* which shatters all structures, forms and concepts.

More and more such metaphors are introduced: fear is represented in images, and *angst* or anxiety can be felt only tentatively, as a strange undercurrent to the linguistic imagery. But this very transfer of anxiety phenomena to other areas, the substitution of feared objects for anxiety, means that no overall pattern into which all the disparate images might be integrated will evolve. This furthers the expansive openness of the textual structures; anxiety itself, however, is not communicable by just being referred to.

Here the difference between *angst* as an emotional dimension of human existence and anxiety in literature shows up clearly; the use of imagery does not wholly solve this problem of incommensurability. Only such metaphors as relate to the symptoms of anorexia nervosa, or the phantasm of the dismembered body, carry subliminal connotations of disgust and paralysis. These alien ideas *are* able to engender, through their interaction with the other textual strategies, the openness which can tip over into a sense of oppression. Existential *angst* and anxiety as a component of psychoses, however, resist both language and literature.

Anxiety is also at the centre of Doris Lessing's *The Golden Notebook* (New York, 1962). The novel is about the search for identity, the loss of identity and a slowly developing mental illness which finally leads up to a psychotic personality dissolution. Identity is usually effected by the unification of present and past experience. Now, an integral factor of our everyday experience is the multiplicity of widely differing roles that we are forced to play. They are either socially or emotionally conditioned; some must be played consecutively and some simultaneously. Often, the heterogeneity of our various roles and the contradictions among them make it difficult to achieve a unified identity. As soon as we reject some of the social roles available, however, and try to devise new ones, the process becomes extremely problematical.

An example of a struggle for identity that is fraught with precarious conflicts is the topic of *The Golden Notebook*: the life of the protagonist, Anna Wulf, is divided into a multiplicity of roles, many of which she accepts – for instance, those of mother and friend – but many of which she utterly rejects, experimenting instead with alternative lifestyles; particularly as writer and mistress, she attempts to redefine the roles available to her, thus opposing both herself and her environment. She tries out other, new roles, relinquishing them again after a while: roles, for instance, that result from her commitment to the Communist Party, or roles allotted to her through her psychoanalysis. In the course of the novel, Anna Wulf becomes less and less able to integrate these heterogeneous roles with her past. Almost inevitably, her search for identity ends in psychosis.

Not only is the multiplicity of the protagonist's roles the topic of the novel, this multiplicity is also contained in the novel's formal structure: much the greater part of *The Golden Notebook* is written from the protagonist's point of view. In this respect there is a striking parallel with the narrative perspective of *Der Hunger nach Wahnsinn*. As opposed to Erlenberger's protagonist, however, Anna Wulf is writing not one but five different books, in five different perceptual modes, being obviously unable to accommodate her fragmenting consciousness in a single text. This division into various heterogeneous perspectives on the plot is one of the textual strategies that prestructure the reader's response, and one that is an idiosyncratic feature of this novel.

*The Golden Notebook* contains the literary device of 'books within a book'. This technique is nothing new or innovative in itself; it was employed by literary texts as early as Geoffrey Chaucer's *Canterbury Tales* (1387) or Giovanni Boccaccio's *Decameron* (1351). In our times, this device for regulating aesthetic distance and, by doing so, the reader's involvement in the text has even been taken over by the cinema. In the movies, as in literature, thematizing the fictionality of various stories that are to be included in a frame narrative (or a frame film) aims first and foremost at authenticating whatever is depicted. Christian Metz writes: 'There are . . . those "films within a film" which downgear the mechanism of our belief–unbelief and anchor it in several stages, hence more strongly: the included film was an illusion, so the including film (the film as such) was not, or was somewhat less so.'[20] Through the device of 'books within a book', a literary text is – paradoxical as it may seem – made plausible by intensification of its fictional dimension.

*The Golden Notebook*, however, does not come into the 'books within a book' category, or at least not in any simple and unmitigated way. The literary convention is subverted, in that it is deprived of its usual effect, which consists in authenticating the frame narrative. There is no hierarchy between the books; thus, the narrative frame does not dominate the other perspectives, but is of equal status and value to all the other books (that is, to the individual and separate perspectives) which are juxtaposed as if at random.[21] What at first seems to lend itself to an easy reception process is the very condition for bringing about unusual and interesting responses.

The individual conflicting perspectives are so diversified that they cannot even be synchronized by a plot, which usually gains plausibility by developing in time. As opposed to any reading process which is almost always linear and directed towards the end of the text in question, the plot of *The Golden Notebook* is circular and directed to the beginning. This rather curious phenomenon is signalled by the four different openings of the narrative. Parallel stages of plot development are opened up by and attached to each new beginning. In compliance with these four openings, the novel falls into four successive cycles; each of these subdivisions contains sections of a rather conventional story entitled 'Free Women'. Only the end of the book discloses that this story constitutes a 'core novel' for which passages from four different 'Notebooks' were to provide 'the raw material'.

In the 'Free Women' sections, episodes from Anna Wulf's life in London during the years 1957 and 1958 are described in chronological order and in a detached, ironic manner. The 'Notebooks', on the other hand, are written as first-person narratives similar to a diary, covering the years 1950–7; sometimes they run parallel to the plot of the 'Free Women' story, sometimes they report events from farther back in time. Towards the end of

*The Golden Notebook* the pattern of the four large narrative blocks breaks up. The last part of the novel consists of yet another perspective, the 'Golden Notebook', which leads into the final episode of the 'Free Women' story. In *The Golden Notebook*, form is not an overall and certainly not an integrating structure: it is divided into a number of perspectives, which cannot be unified by the narrator's consciousness – the subject of the novel itself, indeed, is the struggle for such a unification.[22]

Thus, neither the overall formal structure nor the consciousness of the protagonist can serve as the reader's centre of orientation and anchor his mental images. That means that during the reading process, no integration of the disparate elements can be achieved. The 'books within a book' device is devoid of its function of authenticating the narrative because it fails to establish a hierarchy. Each of the textual perspectives stands on its own, and offers a different way of understanding and interpreting the work by referring to philosophical concepts beyond the text – psychoanalysis, Marxism, literature.

Within the different textual perspectives into which *The Golden Notebook* is divided, the subject matter is presented in those modes of discourse appropriate to psychoanalysis, Marxism and literature. Of course, there is always the danger of linguistic erosion as soon as something is expressed in a form of discourse which is taken for granted and might even border on jargon. In Doris Lessing's novel, the cliché-ridden nature of any jargon becomes the prerequisite for allowing differences of style to emerge as a textual strategy.

The 'Red Notebook', for instance, is about Anna Wulf's commitment to the British Communist Party. It contains comments on its political work, and an implicit criticism of the official party line which is conveyed by parody. The context to which the remarks of the 'Red Notebook' refer is created by Marxist philosophy and its translation into party politics:

By-election. North London. Candidates – Conservative, Labour, Communist. A Labour seat, but with a reduced majority from the previous election. As usual, long discussions in C.P. circles about whether it is right to split the Labour vote. I've been in on several of them. These discussions have the same pattern. No, we don't want to split the vote; it's essential to have Labour in, rather than a Tory. But on the other hand, if we believe in C.P. policy, we must try to get our candidate in. Yet we know there's no hope of getting a C.P. candidate in. This impasse remains until emissary from Centre comes in to say that it's wrong to see the C.P. as a kind of ginger group, that's just defeatism, we have to fight the election as if we were convinced we were going to win it. (But we know we aren't going to win it.) So the fighting speech by the man from Centre,

while it inspires everyone to work hard, does not resolve the basic
dilemma. On the three occasions I watched this happen, the doubts
and confusions were solved by – *a joke*. (p. 164)[23]

Apart from the critical and ironic undertone, this description is marked by
its use of short, precise sentences, reminiscent of party jargon. There is
nothing superfluous; in some places even the definite article is omitted
('until emissary from Centre comes'). The style is ponderous and dogmatic, and is characterized – like the type of Marxism to which it relates –
by its positive, stabilizing effect, which proceeds from the comfortable
certainty that all phenomena can be explained by means of one philosophical concept.

The 'Blue Notebook' deals with everyday events in diary form. Anna
Wulf's life is dominated by the necessity of looking after her daughter
Janet. The contingency of her daily life is projected on to the structuring
system of psychoanalysis. The protagonist undergoes psychoanalytic
treatment and gives a detailed account of all its vicissitudes. Her motive
for seeing a (Jungian) psychoanalyst is her strong desire to overcome a
writer's block. (Although she thinks of herself as a writer, she has published no more than a single novel.) This textual perspective is almost
completely dominated by the way in which psychoanalysis would interpret our world and our actions.

It was then I decided to use the blue notebook, this one, as nothing
but a record of facts. Every evening I sat on the music-stool and
wrote down my day, and it was as if I, Anna, were nailing Anna to
the page. Every day I shaped Anna, said: Today I got up at seven,
cooked breakfast for Janet, sent her to school etc. etc., and felt as if I
had saved that day from chaos. Yet now I read those entries and feel
nothing . . . Words mean nothing. They have become, *when I
think*, not the form into which experience is shaped, but a series of
meaningless sounds, like nursery talk, and away to one side of
experience. Or like the sound track of a film that has slipped its
connection with the film . . . So I can't write any longer. Or only
when I write fast, without looking back at what I have written. For if
I look back, then the words swim and have no sense and I am
conscious only of me, Anna, as a pulse in a great darkness, and the
words that I, Anna, write down are nothing. (p. 476)

This passage is paradigmatic of the way in which, in the 'Blue Notebook',
hidden connections of meaning are sought, with obvious sensitivity, in
everyday life, and then worked through with an amazing amount of
self-reflection. Anna Wulf thus activates the very qualities that are to be
brought about in psychoanalysis.

The 'Black Notebook' circles around Anna Wulf's one published novel. It is subdivided into two parts: 'Money', a listing of the financial transactions necessary in connection with the publication of her novel, and 'Source', an attempt to grasp those 'real' occurrences and events that the narrator sees as the basis of her novel, from a considerable temporal distance and without the dreaded 'false nostalgia' she constantly conjures up. The 'Black Notebook' documents the way in which the narrating ego slips deeper and deeper into psychotic hallucinations, and ends with a confused assortment of newspaper cuttings about current political affairs. The eventual abandoning of Anna Wulf's own writing in favour of newspaper cuttings emphasizes the protagonist's inability to take this textual perspective any further: her silence lingers very noticeably behind the apparent objectivity of printed material and weighs it down.

The textual perspective of the 'Black Notebook', about the transformation of life into literature, is complemented by the 'Yellow Notebook'. This notebook experiments with the conventions of fiction. To signal fictionality in the context of a literary text, a novel, calls for special techniques and devices. In *The Golden Notebook*, literature is set up in analogy to Marxism and psychoanalysis. Through the highlighting of the sequential relationship of Marxism, psychoanalysis and literature, literature too can function as a frame of reference. This is quite unusual for a literary text, to say the least of it. In the Black and Yellow Notebooks literature, like Marxism and psychoanalysis, serves as an organized system of thought potent enough to structure whatever contingencies might be encountered. But, unlike Marxism and its dogmatic rigidity on the one hand, and psychoanalysis with its subtle influence on individual attitudes to life on the other, fictionality has no attribute that could be conveyed by the use of a particular style. Therefore this specific system of thought cannot simply be conjured up by the use of a certain style of discourse (of whatever kind).

In the Black and Yellow Notebooks, the protagonist tries to convert into literature those events which, in the Red and the Blue Notebooks, she has already endowed with patterns and interpretations. Her interpretative patterns derive their meaning from the frame of reference dominating each respective notebook. In the Black and Yellow Notebooks, the protagonist's attempt to mould life into literature fails again and again. Her literary style deteriorates. Eventually, it appears a mere playing with words, unable to transmit the impact of the narrated events.

Every attempt to shape, structure and interpret life necessarily entails a reduction of complexity. Therefore, narrated reality is always, to a certain degree, falsified reality. All experience, when verbalized, is shaped and interpreted, even more so when verbalized in literary language. In the

Black and Yellow Notebooks, this phenomenon is taken to its extremes: the narrator's reality is conveyed in a sterile, falsifying way.

Paradoxically, it is again the sequential relationship between the Black and Yellow versus the Red and Blue Notebooks that transmits the narrator's inability to transform life into literature. The processes of verbalization and reduction that occur between Anna Wulf's daily life on the one hand, and the Red and Blue Notebooks on the other, highlight the deficiencies of the two textual perspectives centred on fictionality, and their ultimate failure to fulfil their intentions.

The disintegration of these four separate perspectives, which stand for separate areas in the protagonist's life, finally and almost of necessity leads into an acute psychotic attack. After this phase of extreme self-confrontation,[24] Anna Wulf believes she can synthesize her life, disintegrated as it is into separate parts, into a single prose text which she calls 'The Golden Notebook'. The opening sentence of this prose text runs: 'The two women were alone in a London flat'; the first part of the 'Free Women' sequence (and with it the novel *The Golden Notebook*) begins with the same sentence too. Only at this point – very late in the novel – does it become clear that the individual instalments of the 'Free Women' story (that is, the fifth textual perspective in which the plot is presented) are meant to represent yet another account of what the protagonist has set down apparently at random in her diaries.

The literary device idiosyncratic of Lessing's novel – 'books within a book' – forms a non-hierarchical sequence of four different narrative cycles. Each cycle contains alternate instalments of all five textual perspectives which, in turn, depict events in Anna Wulf's life in pointedly different linguistic styles. The various levels of discourse imply a change in attitudes. The way in which the five textual perspectives interlock and form a sequence seems to suggest that events from Anna Wulf's past, as narrated in her notebooks, provide both the material and the interpretation of present events. But even if the individual notebooks are arranged in a repetitive pattern, thematically they highlight first and foremost the inconsistencies between the individual perspectives. Their subject matter does not fall into a unified pattern, and defies all attempts at integration: Anna Wulf keeps re-reading her notebooks, trying to define and stabilize her own identity by encountering her past. Trying to integrate her experience, however, leads her to ever greater psychic fragmentation.

Integration is impossible, and not just for the protagonist: the reader cannot connect up the disparate data either. The various discourses and the different events that form the basis of the five textual perspectives begin to interact, and yet no coherent pictures emerges. Stories that have been broken off are suddenly taken up again, given a new twist and handled from different angles. Their temporal and logical connections are tangled and obscured. John L. Carey writes:

> We must wonder why in 1957, in the first 'Free Women' section, Tommy is twenty years old (*GN*, p. 13) and in a notebook written in 1950 he is seventeen (*GN*, p. 197). Why, too, at the end of the 'Free Women' sections are we told that Tommy goes off to Sicily with Marion, Richard's second wife (*GN*, p. 554), while in the notebooks he marries a younger girl (*GN*, p. 468)? Why are Molly, Anna, Richard and Tommy referred to by the same names in the notebooks as well as in the 'Free Women' sections and Saul Green, Anna's lover in the notebooks, called 'Milt' in the 'Free Women' sections? Why is the account of Saul's relationship with Anna so much less developed in the final 'Free Women' section than in the notebooks?[25]

The 'Free Women' sections cover a period of about a year, while the notebooks extend over seven years and sometimes refer to events even further back. The sequence of the separate notebooks does run according to a fixed – if apparently arbitrary – pattern (a 'Free Women' section is always followed by sections from the Black, Red, Yellow and Blue Notebooks), but different amounts of space are allotted to the various sections, and though the sequence is fixed, it is not necessarily the same events that are treated in them.

As the reading process, by definition, occurs along a linear time axis, the cyclical course of the narrative, which is directed towards ever new beginnings, makes great demands on the reader's combinatory capacities. Moreover, events occurring at various points in time have to be synchronized. The recipient is obliged to play an active part in carrying out the very process of reducing complexity which is highlighted again and again by the narrator's difficulties in transforming her life into literature. By means of his own projections and phantasies, the reader participates in the protagonist's attempt to create identity out of contradictory incidents and experiences. His reading aims – as all reading does – at building consistency, and in order to build consistency he himself must provide the missing links between the separate but interacting textual perspectives. Paradoxically, the literary device of 'books within a book' – despite its apparent conventionality – instigates a reader-response that takes on a high degree of immediacy. In *The Golden Notebook*, the impossibility of achieving a well-grounded identity is transposed into the reading process and informs the interaction between text and reader.[26]

The reader's reactions oscillate. At the beginning of the reading process, they are predominantly cognitive and pleasant; the synchronization of disparate plot elements offers intellectual stimulation. However, the reader's attempts to build consistency are doomed to fail; again and again, as the narratives continue, bringing with them further flashbacks, the reader is obliged to modify, revise and finally abandon the mental images he has produced. His failure to make a comprehensive whole out of the disparate fragments is contained in the network of interacting textual perspectives that defy hierarchy. This feature of the formal structure of the text is mirrored by its theme: the writing protagonist's dissociating consciousness, although the centre of organization for all the diverse textual strategies, is unable to achieve integration.

Another interesting feature of the reader-response contained in this novel consists in the phenomenon that the reader's initially pleasurable reactions are gradually modified in the course of the reading process. The way in which the protagonist deals with her own problems is of crucial significance for effecting this change in response. Anna Wulf is continually splitting off the negative traits in her character (or projecting them on others); moreover, she stages what for her is a destructive pattern of relationships again and again.

The material that the protagonist has split off and repressed surfaces in the dreams she discusses in her sessions of Jungian psychoanalysis. One dream sequence, which Anna Wulf dreams frequently, with slight variations, centres upon a single figure, an old man who suffers from a handicap:

> This old man smiled and giggled and sniggered, was ugly, vital and powerful, and again, what he represented was pure spite, malice, joy in malice, joy in a destructive impulse . . . The element took a variety of shapes, usually that of a very old man or woman . . . and the figure was always very lively, in spite of having a wooden leg, or a crutch, or a hump, or being deformed in some way. And the creature was always powerful, with an inner vitality which I knew was caused by a purposeless, undirected, causeless spite. It mocked and jibed and hurt, wished murder, wished death. And yet it was always vibrant with joy. (pp. 477f)

In the course of her psychoanalytic treatment, the protagonist is asked to give this dream a name. She says at first it is 'the nightmare about destruction' (p. 477), and then calls it 'the nightmare about the principle of spite, or malice – joy in spite' (p. 477). Her analyst is not satisfied; she wants Anna to see the ambivalence of this dream figure: 'She enquired: "Only negative qualities, nothing good about it?" "Nothing," I said, surprised. "And there is nothing creative at all there?" "Not for me" ' (p. 478). The protagonist cannot acknowledge this figure – which, as an antithetic combination of vitality and malice, is a typical product of the primary process (in which opposites are condensed into a single entity) – as a negative trait of her own psyche. She splits it off completely and defines it as a neutral quality which is totally alien to her nature. Subsequently, she breaks off her psychoanalysis without having worked through the negative elements in her psyche.

The figure, or rather the vital element contained in the figure, suddenly appears again in another area of her life, one which seems to have nothing in common with her psychoanalysis. (This rather strange incident conforms to the psychoanalytic axiom that psychic conflicts which have not been worked through and integrated into the ego are subject to an unconscious repetition compulsion.) The protagonist and her lover, who also has ambitions as a writer, exchange first lines for a literary text. Thereupon the protagonist writes the first instalment of the 'Free Women' sequence, and her lover a short novel about an Algerian soldier. Anna Wulf reads, interprets and summarizes her lover's text. Her résumé of his short novel (p. 642) displays a quality of vital cruelty engendering an atmosphere strikingly similar to that of the dream sequence quoted above. At the end of her résumé, she states: 'This short novel was later published and did rather well' (p. 643). Anna Wulf ascribes the authorship of this (her) text to someone else, her lover Saul Green. She translates the negative elements contained in her psyche, those which appear in ever-changing form in her nightmares, into the literary discourse of her notebooks: the summary is hers, not his. Thus she completely dissociates some of her own negative qualities from herself. She is using writing as defence, as a mechanism for fending off self-confrontation.

The dissociative state of the protagonist's consciousness – which has already been documented by the fading out of two of the textual perspectives into the sterility of newspaper cuttings – finally leads into an acute psychotic attack, with Saul Green as initiator and participant. In her relationship with her lover, again, Anna Wulf blocks out certain vital facets: she intentionally refuses to perceive what is going on: 'I noted there was a touch of sullenness as he said it, but I chose not to hear it' (p. 561). She repeatedly observes that it is he who is going through a psychotic attack, while she, she says, was only drawn into it with him. She detects in Saul Green the presence of a sickness which she calls an 'anxiety state' and which, as it does not seem to be her own, she can analyse soberly, at a distance: 'Well, I'll never suffer from my own anxiety state, so I might as well experience someone else's while I get the chance' (p. 575).[27] The fact that in so doing she is merely acting out her familiar defence mechanism becomes clearer and clearer in the course of her description: 'The malicious irresponsible principle was embodied in Saul. Throughout a long nightmare it had taunted me laughing. It had held me tight by the arms so I couldn't move and said: "I'm going to hurt you. I enjoy it" ' (p. 579). The protagonist is projecting not only her present emotional anxiety state on to Saul Green, but also her own negative personality traits. This projection intensifies to the point at which the protagonist begins to perceive the dyadic interaction between Saul Green and herself as the interplay of several completely different personalities.

> What was strange was, that the man who had said No, defending his freedom, and the man who said, pleading, It doesn't mean anything, were two men. I couldn't connect them. I was silent, in the grip of apprehension again, and then a third man said, brotherly and affectionate: 'Go to sleep now.'
>
> I went to sleep, in obedience to this third friendly man, conscious of two other Annas, separate from the obedient child – Anna, the snubbed woman in love, cold and miserable in some corner of myself, and a curious detached sardonic Anna, looking on and saying: 'Well, well!' (p. 562)

Anna Wulf experiences all the phenomena characteristic of psychotic attacks, such as sensing her physical boundaries (p. 612) and her conception of a space–time continuum dissolve. An illusion of being possessed by others also, and increasingly, comes to the fore; it seems to be strongly linked to her communication with Saul Green. Together, they stage all kinds of different situations, constantly changing roles.

> I was playing roles, one after another, against Saul, who was playing roles. It was like being in a play, whose words kept changing, as if a playwright had written the same play again and again, but slightly different each time. We played against each other every man–woman role imaginable. As each cycle . . . came to an end, I said: 'Well, I've experienced that, have I, well it was time that I did'. It was like living a hundred lives. (pp. 603f)

Anna Wulf and Saul Green are entangled in a highly symbiotic relationship, in a never-flagging cycle of aggression, cruelty, jealousy, guilt and passion; their two personalities seem to merge almost entirely: 'Then there was a moment of knowledge. I understood I'd gone . . . right inside his craziness . . . I understood I could no longer separate myself from Saul, and that frightened me more than I have been frightened' (p. 587).

Time and again, Anna Wulf's psychotic experience rises to an intensity in which she is no longer capable of perceiving and relating to her world, although she can still take fragmentary notes about what is going on (pp. 599f). Her psychotic attack comes to an abrupt end when her daughter returns from boarding school and Saul Green leaves her. The question of whether she was able to initiate a return from the world of psychotic experience herself, and was thus in control of her psychotic episode, is left open. Moreover, the fact that the novel ends here allows no conclusions about any possible changes for the better. Will she subsequently be able to achieve an integration of her divergent personality traits?

The protagonist's writing initially served her as a defence mechanism, and during the description of her psychotic attack it becomes a guarantee that she will never move dangerously far from the area she perceives as normality. Through writing about herself and her psychotic condition, she stabilizes herself by the magic powers of her own invocations. Even at moments of the most intense delusion, she refuses to project any image of herself other than that of a woman who can still master the rules of syntax, spelling and punctuation. (Similarly, she describes herself in the 'Free Women' sections as an almost boringly normal woman without any inclination to consciousness-raising, phantasies or delusions.)

The protagonist's self-image is of crucial significance for the fact that a new dimension is added to the reader's response while processing the text. The protagonist's psychotic attack is first mentioned in the Yellow Notebook (centred on the transformation of life into literature); the actual account of her psychotic experience occurs in the Blue Notebook, where Anna Wulf describes her everyday life in a rather conventional style. Obviously, the protagonist's psychic fragmentation is so far advanced that she is no longer able to perform the fictionalizing activity of reshaping everyday life in literary discourse by playing with different perspectives. (The Yellow Notebook is based on this fictionalizing activity.) The lack of divergent perspectives, however, considerably simplifies the plot of the novel. The narrator ceases to re-work and correct what she has already described: the vibrating network of multidimensional textual perspectives is suddenly abandoned in favour of an almost sterile, linear account. Subsequently, the psychotic episode takes on the stifling form of a stereotype. It has a similar impact, in a way, to the rigidly one-dimensional style of narration employed in the 'Free Women' sections.

## Aesthetic response in the literary type of psychopathography

Reading *The Golden Notebook*, the reader must at first actively supplement his mental images by fictionalizing acts similar to those that occur between the separate notebooks. Setting his intellectual capacities into motion makes him experience the reading as creative, stimulating and pleasurable. The fact that certain positions in the text and the turn of the plot repeatedly force him to abandon his fictionalizations may give rise to slight pangs of irritation, but they are absorbed without much trouble into the more pleasurable aspects of the reading process.

As reading continues, however, the frustrating factors become more and more dominant. On the thematic level of the novel, this has already been anticipated by the conversion of two of the notebooks into a series of newspaper cuttings. Finally, all textual perspectives are compressed into a single schematized narration, the linear account of the psychotic experience. Both the topic of the novel and the eventual stylistic simplification of its textual strategies affect the reader's aesthetic response. After all, the protagonist's mental dissociations offer the reader a centre of orientation for holding the various diverse aspects and schemata in the novel together, if only insufficiently. The apparent necessity with which these dissociations lead into psychosis, and the repetitive exploding of the plot through re-directing it to the beginning, combine forces and heighten the reader's frustration and irritation; they may even become tainted with a sense of oppression. The previous, more pleasurable ways of interacting with the text now constitute a frame of reference by way of retrospection. This frame of reference – rather unstable in itself – highlights the twists and turns in the reader's response to the text as he moves away from a sphere of stimulating imaginative activity and gradually slides into one of frustration and oppression.

The reader's response oscillates between pleasure and 'unpleasure';[28] yet this pattern is subject to considerable changes in the course of the reading process: when he starts reading, the recipient has what are mainly pleasurable interactions with the text, interactions which are occasionally interrupted by oscillatory deviations towards realms tainted with the irritant. From approximately the middle of the novel onwards, the stylistically much-simplified mode of narration and representation causes the reception process to be experienced as predominantly irritant or frustrating. Even here the processing of the text, which is characterized by negative and frustrating dimensions, does not take a linear course, but is interrupted by individually based impulses of counter-control (reminiscences of more pleasurable reading experiences).

The theme of *The Golden Notebook* is a struggle to establish identity, one which ultimately leads to complete loss of identity. The protagonist's ego boundaries become blurred; her seemingly stable personality profile is dissolved. A psychosis contains both negative and positive aspects. It is usually experienced as a state of great anxiety; however, at the same time a certain amount of creativity may surface during such a human borderline experience. The ambivalence of a psychosis is mirrored in the specific pattern of the oscillations between pleasure and unpleasure contained in the reader's response. A loss of identity has positive and creative aspects, and similarly the pattern of the reader's reactions displays positive and pleasurable aspects too. The negativity involved in self-loss, on the other hand, is conveyed through those instances in the formal structure of the text which give rise to pangs of irritation and frustration when the reader is processing them. The ambivalence of psychotic experience, with both its pleasurable and its frustrating elements, is thus staged in the interplay of text and reader.

In *Der Hunger nach Wahnsinn*, the literary device of two separate levels of presentation, the interchangeability of textual segments and endless repetitions which are of great linguistic but slight semantic variability, combine forces and turn the textual strategies into entities which seem to expand boundlessly. Openness and expansion are further intensified by an assimilation of textual strategies taken over from the genre of mediating texts, with the reading habits such texts induce (the expectation of a stabilizing reading experience) being both called upon and subverted. In conjunction with literary discourse in which disgust, paralysis and anxiety are not spelled out but subliminally evoked (by means of specific imagery), the openness contained in the reader's response may implode into a sense of oppression.

Thus, in the two novels analysed here, certain emotional aspects of psychoses are staged in the reader's emotional involvement with the text; he reacts emotionally to something not linguistically manifest in the text, although it is prestructured by the interplay of all the textual strategies.

Psychopathographies call on the *reading habits* formed through reading series of mediating texts, a reading habit which is characterized mainly by the expectation of stabilizing reading experiences. They are anchored in both the formal structures of mediating texts, which are relatively easy to process, and their overall ability to balance deficits. Psychopathographies play on these expectations: reference is made to the possibility of stabilizing reading experiences by taking over textual strategies from the genre of mediating texts, but at the same time they are subverted and ultimately rejected. However, it is first and foremost the theme of the novel in question, generally transposed into linguistic discourse by the use of an idiosyncratic literary device – a specific imagery in the case of *Der Hunger nach Wahnsinn*, and the convention of 'books within a book' in *The Golden Notebook* – that intensifies the expansive openness of the reading process to such an extent that it may even tip over into a sense of oppression: the subject-matter, the depiction of a psychosis, arouses a multitude of individually based phantasies.

In mediating texts, a specific constellation of literary strategies – which in themselves are rather sterile and negate most of the options open to literary discourse – and the strong emphasis laid on the one central perspective from which the plot is presented, have a sociocultural function. This textual pattern offers an opportunity for mediating texts to intervene in group processes. Assimilating well-established and much-used textual strategies into a new aesthetic context – like, for instance, psychopathographic texts – does not automatically mean that the specific function of these strategies will be transferred too. Both genres do indeed take human experiences as their subject. Where, in mediating texts, these are peculiar to and consitutive of certain groups, psychopathographic texts are about psychotic experiences which defy discourse; psychotic experiences are far from being shared by groups whose function is a primarily sociopolitical one. There is no group feeling upon which psychopathographic texts may touch.[29]

# 4

# The theoretical type of psychopathography

Literary texts are not the only ones to react to the language problem posed by those phenomena that elude discourse. There is a certain kind of *theoretical* text which also deals with such phenomena, and which therefore is also forced to develop new strategies of representation and communication: psychoanalytically orientated case histories attempt to establish that psychoses are amenable to treatment. On the one hand, they take as their subject the way in which explosively instinctual, unconscious material – which threatens the ego boundaries – can or rather should be integrated into the psychotherapeutic process, thus bringing the therapist's interpretations and interventions into view, while on the other hand they must simultaneously convey that dimension of actual and subjective experience shared by psychotherapist and patient within which the intended personality changes will occur. Good psychotherapies (like good psychoanalyses) are of their nature a balancing act between limiting factors (the structuring of the therapeutic process initiated by the therapist) and expanding factors (the processes of transference and counter-transference).[1] As psychoanalytically orientated case histories must take these singularly antagonistic forces into account, the representation of such processes in theoretical texts would seem difficult, to say the least.

Moreover, case histories are confronted with additional problems of discourse occasioned by their specific subject: psychotherapies and psychoanalyses consist largely of the analysand's personal narratives. As opposed to psychotic episodes which resist verbalization, psychoanalytic therapy relies almost entirely on the communicatory functions of language. A compulsion to verbalize every thought and feeling the very moment it arises forms the basis of therapy, its 'fundamental rule'.[2] Language in the context of such treatment, however, is of no interest in itself; it is deprived of its communicatory potency and becomes a mere vehicle for processes of resistance, defence, transference and counter-transference, in fact for the subjective and expanding factors in a therapy.

Those very phenomena – contained in and communicated by linguistic processes – defy description in theoretical discourse. Freud himself observed that it did not suffice to publish accounts of conversation in psychoanalytic situations:

> It is well known that no means has been found of in any way introducing into the reproduction of an analysis the sense of conviction which results from the analysis itself. Exhaustive verbatim reports of the proceedings during the hours of analysis would certainly be of no help at all; and in any case the technique of the treatment makes it impossible to draw them up.[3]

The fact that a therapy is based almost exclusively on verbal exchanges between an analysand and a therapist does not, paradoxically, make it more amenable to written discourse. Rather, conversation in the therapeutic situation or, to be more precise, the semantic dimension of that conversation, presents an additional problem: an account, in fragmentary form, has to be given of the outward history of the patient's life as well as of the inner, psychic condition of his conflicts. During therapy, the latter is linked with the revelation, going farther and farther back into his life history, of those factors which caused his manifest symptoms; this uncovering is the *thematic* basis of every therapy. That, however, means that there are two times axes running counter to each other: a progressive, biographical and a regressive, therapeutically determined time sequence must both be documented. In case histories, consequently, we are confronted (so far as their representation of time is concerned) with a kind of *double* historiography.

The aims of the case history as a form of theoretical discourse, which I have only briefly outlined so far – the description of structuring and expanding elements, together with the documentation of one progressive and one regressive time axis, that is to say, of two different, antagonistic factors – lead to my hypothesis that psychoanalytic case histories draw upon and integrate narrative patterns of representation in order to meet those linguistic requirements.[4] That could mean that a theoretical form of discourse reacts to the problem of having to communicate a phenomenon which defies communication by assimilating literary devices, thus moving closer to literary discourse.

Historically speaking, psychoanalytic case histories developed from the necessity of communicating to those who had not themselves participated in a specific therapy what can occur in psychoanalytic processes, as well as pointing out the relevance to psychoanalytic theory and technique of the psychic material on which this specific therapy was based. Because of their target group, the relatively narrow circle of analysts and students of psychoanalysis, and because of their intermediate position (as I postulate it here) between purely theoretical metapsychological texts[5] (studies such as Freud's essay on 'The Ego and the Id'[6]) and narrative texts, I will draw an analogy between psychoanalytic case histories and the theoretical type of mediating text: if the latter offers a particular social group a theoretical foundation (one upon which its objectives and, in turn, the establishment of group identity are based), then case histories attempt to convey the conditions of psychotherapy, within a discourse which claims to be theoretical, to a target audience whose conception of itself as a group depends on learning such matters.

As the antagonistic processes occurring during therapy fall into the category of phenomena that are hard to communicate, and it is difficult, to say the least, to verbalize them, the learning of psychoanalytic technique turns out to be fraught with problems. The individual reception of case histories plays a central part in any attempt to acquire psychoanalytic technique: in training seminars, group discussions of such texts take place – and here again we have a parallel to mediating texts. The fundamental difference between psychoanalytic case histories and mediating texts, however, lies in the fact that their subject matter potentially defies *theoretical* documentation. Because of the way they react to a problem of discourse – which links them to the literary type of psychopathography – I will classify and analyse case histories as the theoretical type of psychopathography.

## The conventions of psychoanalytic case histories

I chose the writings of Frieda Fromm-Reichmann for testing my hypothesis that psychoanalytic case histories contain features of literary discourse; however, I will also discuss Freud's case histories, which provide the basic framework for the genre, for purposes of contrast.[7] Freud's and Fromm-Reichmann's case histories differ in that Freud wrote long, continuous narratives, a combination of his notes about a case and an account of his psychoanalytic research, which were to serve as evidence of the validity of his psychoanalytic axioms. With the psychoanalytic writings of Freud's successors, the form of the case history (as developed by Freud) gradually changed. A convention emerged of inserting short fragments from actual cases into theoretical treatises, and signalling the fact that these were interpolations in another type of discourse by the use of a different typeface; today, this convention is well established, and is clearly visible in Fromm-Reichmann's texts.

My reason for selecting Fromm-Reichmann's texts in particular for textual analysis, out of all the many case histories that have been published, is a historical coincidence of great interest in the context of this study: two extremely different texts, which may be classified within the psychopathography genre as belonging to the theoretical type and the imitative type of text respectively, take the therapeutic treatment of the same psychosis as the occasion for their writing: *I Never Promised You a Rose Garden* (1964) by Hannah Green (the pseudonym of Joanne Greenberg) is a novel dealing with the identical case referred to by Fromm-Reichmann in several essays written in 1952–7, where she set out the theoretical basis of her concept of a psychoanalytically orientated therapy of psychosis.

In that a patient uses the creative energies set free by psychotherapy to transform his therapeutic and/or psychotic experiences into a novel, or even just an account of analysis, the case of Fromm-Reichmann and Greenberg shows an interesting parallel to that of Freud and one of his patients, the 'Wolf-Man': in 1918 Freud wrote an article 'From the History of an Infantile Neurosis',[8] based on his treatment of the Wolf-Man. Subsequently, the Wolf-Man himself wrote a record of his analyses.[9] (Apart from his analysis with Freud – which is considered by modern psychoanalysis to have been ineffective and in the final resort a failure[10] – the Wolf-Man later had treatment with Ruth Mack Brunswick in order to work through elements of his unresolved transference to Freud.) Many analysands have given accounts of their training analyses. These writings are chiefly motivated by the interest of decoding the Freudian technique of treatment.[11] Probably the best known of such studies is H.D.'s *Tribute to Freud* (New York, 1956); a later and more spectacular work is Tilman Moser's *Years of Apprenticeship on the Couch: Fragments of my Psychoanalysis* (New York, 1977); Moser, of course, was not in analysis with Freud himself. However, we have only a few accounts of analyses which were begun because of mental illness rather than for training purposes.[12]

In the context of this study, the writings of Fromm-Reichmann in particular suggest themselves for textual analysis because she belongs to that generation of post-Freudian analysts that made schizoid personality disorders accessible to psychoanalytic treatment by developing a therapy diverging from the classic technique.

*All* psychoanalytically orientated case histories – those that rely upon the classic therapeutic technique as well as those that contain a modified concept of treatment – must describe both expanding *and* structuring elements, both progressive *and* regressive time axes. The communication of such opposing forces is usually achieved by narrative forms of discourse. Throughout history, narrative has always been an important component of those types of discourse that aim to explain, convince and instruct. The specifically *didactic* function of case histories (that element which links them to the genre of mediating texts) seems to suggest if not demand the communication of therapeutic data by means of narrative devices. In modern literature, however, the ability of narrative to explain our world (or even just to represent it) is questioned again and again.[13] If case histories adopt narrative elements, I assume that they must also necessarily take account of the fact that in our time narrative discourse is regarded as suspicious and problematical.

### The 'Wolf-Man' analysis as a problem of discourse

The personal narratives of analysands resist mimetic depiction in theoretical discourse, since of their nature they are disordered. Part of the work of psychoanalysis consists of filtering out from the patient's incessant and chaotic utterances those elements that can be organized into significant chains of association. Freud writes, in this connection:

> I begin the treatment, indeed, by asking the patient to give me the whole story of his life and illness, but even so the information I receive is never enough to let me see my way about the case. The first account may be compared to an unnavigable river whose stream is at one moment choked by masses of rock and at another divided and lost among shallows and sandbanks. I cannot help wondering how it is that the authorities can produce such smooth and precise histories in cases of hysteria. As a matter of fact the patients are incapable of giving such reports about themselves. They can, indeed, give the physician plenty of coherent information about this or that period of their lives; but it is sure to be followed by another period as to which their communications run dry, leaving gaps unfilled, and riddles unanswered; and then again will come yet another period which will remain totally obscure and unilluminated by even a single piece of serviceable information. The connections – even the ostensible ones – are for the most part incoherent, and the sequence of different events is uncertain. Even during the course of their story patients will repeatedly correct a particular or a date, and then perhaps, after wavering for some time, return to their first version. The patients' inability to give an ordered history of their life in so far as it coincides with the history of their illness is not merely characteristic of the neurosis. It also possesses great theoretical significance. For this inability has the following grounds. In the first place, patients consciously and intentionally keep back part of what they ought to tell – things that are perfectly well known to them – because they have not got over their feelings of timidity and shame . . . this is the share taken by *conscious* disingenuousness. In the second place, part of the anamnestic knowledge, which the patients

have at their disposal at other times, disappears while they are actually telling their story, but without their making any deliberate reservations: the share taken by *unconscious* disingenuousness. In the third place, there are invariably true amnesias – gaps in the memory into which not only old recollections but even quite recent ones have fallen – and paramnesias, formed secondarily so as to fill in those gaps.[14]

Elsewhere,[15] Freud remarks that 'an aversion on the part of the ego' (*Abneigung des Ich*, modern psychoanalysis would use the term 'the ego's unconscious defence mechanisms') has removed the originally pathogenic idea – an experience or a phantasy – from association and suppresses its return. Memories of the same kind are grouped around this pathogenic nucleus. The memories form several layers of resistance displaying similar force, which are condensed and concentrated against the pathogenic nucleus. Only if the resistance is worked through during psychoanalytic treatment and thus made comprehensible can it be linked to its thought content. Ideally, such thought contents form a logical chain, which does not, however, run a linear course, but divides and leads to a converging network of lines. Several trains of thought usually meet together at the same point within this system.

The signs contained in a chain of association are ambivalent in so far as they derive their meaning from an incident rooted in early childhood, and have consequences on the present, consequences in which their original semantic dimension is lost. The disclosure of the original semantic dimension (the pathogenic nucleus) within the therapeutic dialogue means potentially that its negative consequences on the patient's present life might be dissolved.

In their first case histories (the five published in the *Studies on Hysteria*, 1895),[16] Breuer and Freud were still working with the monocausal principle of simply equating a traumatic experience with its continuation in the form of manifest symptoms. This psychoanalytic axiom is also mirrored in the strict and relatively simple linguistic structure of these first case histories. Soon, however, this procedure proved inadequate (psychoanalytically as well as linguistically). Freud himself wrote ten years later, in his case history of 'Dora':[17]

Readers who are familiar with the technique of analysis as it was expounded in the *Studies on Hysteria* will perhaps be surprised that it should not have been possible in three months to find a complete solution at least for those of the symptoms that were taken in hand. This will become intelligible when I explain that since the date of the *Studies* psychoanalytic technique has been completely revolutionized. At that time the work of analysis started out from the symptoms, and aimed at clearing them up one after the other. Since then I have abandoned that technique, because I found it totally inadequate for dealing with the finer structure of a neurosis. I now let the patient himself choose the subject of the day's work, and in that way I start out from whatever surface his unconscious happens to be presenting to his notice at the moment. But on this plan, everything that has to do with the clearing-up of a particular symptom emerges piecemeal, woven into various contexts, and distributed over widely separated periods of time. In spite of this apparent disadvantage, the new technique is far superior to the old.[18]

The procedure sketched out here became more and more complex, and in his treatment of the Wolf-Man Freud had to work his way like an archaeologist (to use one of his favourite metaphors) through many overlapping and intersecting layers of the unconscious to reach its most primitive organizational forms and their defects. Symptoms had several simultaneous meanings which were sometimes expressed consecutively. The chains of significant signs extending between symptoms and dreams and between the various ways of expressing them formed a *structural element*, whereas the Wolf-Man's contingent personal narratives, also significant but – psychoanalytically speaking – incomplete, described his life as it progressed in time.[19]

The characterization given above of the therapeutic factors as an 'integration of opposing time axes' must therefore be reformulated in a specific way, indicating that the phenomenon I am concerned with consists in a relationship of tensions between entities with a spatial and with a temporal structure. To resolve the tension between space and time is a basic human need; many cultural achievements can be interpreted as an attempt to do just this. Frank Kermode, for instance, argues that fictions have always served above all to structure the contingent course of time. Fictions – of all kinds, not just literary ones – correspond to the basic need to regulate time by arbitrarily postulating a beginning and an end. Beginnings and endings impose limits upon the flow of time; thus time can be perceived and experienced as something 'meaning-full'. In his book *The Sense of an Ending* (Oxford, 1966), Kermode calls those fictions that endow their beginnings and endings with a reference to each other, and which thus correspond in a specific way to the human need for the construction of meaningful order, concord fictions: 'Fictions, whose ends are consonant with origins, and in concord, however unexpected, with their precedents, satisfy our needs' (p. 5).

Case histories are such *concord fictions*. The fascination which emanates from psychoanalytic interpretations – that is, from those individual statements which, taken together, form one of the fundamental thematic patterns of case histories (and of psychoanalyses) – can be made plausible by this basic anthropological need: psychoanalytic interpretations occur 'at the end' and integrate the spatial structure of the chain of significant signs with their temporal sequence. Of their nature, then, psychoanalytic interpretations are fictions. Fictions, however, should never be subjected to the question of whether they are true or false; the only question adequate to fictions is that of their function. So what exactly is their function in the analytic process?

In connection with literary plots (which also form a group of concord fictions), Kermode elaborates on another interesting phenomenon: an effort is obviously made to modify the form and content of concord fictions to such effect that the meaningful connection to be constructed between beginning and end is not directly obvious or to be expected. Occurrences of peripeteia, the sudden and unexpected change of circumstances or fortune, play an important part here:

> Peripeteia, which has been called the equivalent, in narrative, of irony in rhetoric, is present in every story of the least structural sophistication. Now peripeteia depends on our confidence of the end; it is a disconfirmation followed by a consonance; the interest of having our expectations falsified is obviously related to our wish to reach the discovery or recognition by an unexpected and instructive route. It has nothing whatever to do with any reluctance on our part to get there at all.[20]

The more complex that the integration of spatial and temporal elements turns out to be, the more they take account of a dynamic momentum (away from the paradigm and towards more open forms), the more fascinating will be its effect and the greater – where case histories are concerned – its power of persuasion and therefore its didactic value.

During his work with the Wolf-Man, Freud was confronted in the psychoanalytic situation with the phenomenon of peripeteia described by Kermode: the Wolf-Man steadfastly resisted Freud's interpretations, thus forcing him to come up with more and more complicated constructions. Now, if one rules out the possibility that the Wolf-Man's behaviour is to be attributed to nothing but resistance (conscious or unconscious), then their interaction shows that Freud's need for concord fictions was obviously answered by a need on the Wolf-Man's part for peripeteia. This curious phenomenon is mirrored in Freud's reflections on the possibilities and limitations of writing up the Wolf-Man story as a case history, for he would and could no longer employ a monocausal pattern of explanation even in written exposition; in the second chapter of the Wolf-Man case history he remarks: 'I am unable to give either a purely historical or a purely thematic account of my patient's story; I can write a history neither of the treatment nor of the illness, but I shall find myself obliged to combine the two methods of presentation.'[21] This combination gave rise to a mode of representation which largely left the linear course of the patient's life story out of consideration, instead stressing the narrative reconstruction of the time sequence during which the intertwinings and superimpositions in the spatially structured chain of significant signs that formed the patient's symptoms were revealed. The characteristics of this specific infantile neurosis, and the chain of significant signs which – by way of extensive circuitous routes – lead to it, determined the course of time during which it was revealed in psychoanalysis. This time sequence is recorded in detail, whereas the patient's life story, upon which the chain of significant signs also has consequences, is mostly neglected.

Freud's individual interpretations, and his case histories as a whole, are – as concord fictions – attempts to integrate spatial and temporal structures. Moreover, they have as their frame of reference a scientific concept: they not only have to bear the burden of proof for the intricacies of psychoanalytic treatment, they must also serve as the ultimate authority from which psychoanalytic theories and techniques of treatment may be derived. However, they do not fulfil either task adequately. Freud was obviously aware of this:

> I must beg the reader to bear in mind that I obtained this history of an infantile neurosis as a by-product, so to speak, during the analysis of an illness in mature years. I have therefore been obliged to put it together from even smaller fragments than are usually at one's disposal for purposes of synthesis. This task, which is not difficult in other respects, finds a natural limit when it is a question of forcing a structure which is itself in many dimensions on to the two-dimensional descriptive plane. I must therefore content myself with bringing forward fragmented portions, which the reader can then put together into a living whole.[22]

Once this 'structure in many dimensions' is subjected to textual analysis, various different 'fragmented portions' can be made out. Classified according to their respective fields of reference, they form three groups, of which:

the first is intended to satisfy the claims of metapsychology (an analysis of the structure underlying the case of infantile neurosis; an account of the constellation of events that led to the infantile neurosis, that is, the aetiology of the neurosis);

the second documents the therapeutic technique (the course of the treatment, that is, an account of the gradual disclosure of the aetiology of the neurosis; the consideration of expanding and limiting factors: the Wolf-Man's resistance[23] and Freud's interpretations);

and the third is determined by the structure of narrative discourse (the organization of the 'raw material' – the account of the therapy, the patient's life story and the aetiology of the neurosis – in a form which makes the raw material look like a 'meaningful' literary plot).

The various 'fragmented portions' are marked in form and content by the specific field of reference from which they arise, that is, by theoretical discourse (metapsychology), narrative discourse (the organization of the material) or an intermediate form between the two (the discussion of psychoanalytic technique). Thus they all relate to fields of reference outside the text. Apart from these connections with realms beyond the text, however, the 'fragmented portions' also have connections with each other, internal connections, which form a peculiar field of tensions: the internal organization of the text contains a perspective system analogous to that described by Iser in *The Act of Reading* with reference to the internal organization of literary texts:

If the function of the different perspectives is to initiate the production of the aesthetic object (i.e., the meaning of the text), it follows that this object cannot be totally represented by any *one* of those perspectives. And while each perspective offers a particular view of the intended object, it also opens up a view on the *other* perspectives. The interaction between perspectives is continuous, because they are not separated distinctly from one another, and they do not run parallel either . . . [they] are interwoven in the text and offer a constantly shifting constellation of views. These, then, are the 'inner' perspectives of the text – to be distinguished from the 'outer' perspective, which links text to outside reality. (p. 96)

And:

As perspectives are continually interweaving and interacting, it is not possible for the reader to embrace all perspectives at once, and so the view he is involved with at any one particular moment is what constitutes for him the 'theme'. This, however, always stands before the 'horizon' of the other perspective segments in which he had previously been situated . . . the structure of theme and horizon organizes the attitudes of the reader and at the same time builds up the perspective system of the text. It is a structure that constitutes the basic rule for the combination of textual strategies . . . It organizes a relationship between text and reader that is essential for comprehension . . . the manner in which he assembles it is dictated by the continual switching of perspectives during the time-flow of his reading, and this, in turn, provides a theme-and-horizon structure which enables him gradually to take over the author's unfamiliar view of the world on the terms laid down by the author. The structure of theme and horizon constitutes the vital link between text and reader, because it actively involves the reader in the process of synthesizing an assembly of constantly shifting viewpoints, which not only modify one another but also influence past and future syntheses.[24]

The claim I made above, that the story narrated in a case history is inadequate to fulfil its function of bearing the burden of proof for the intricacies of psychoanalytic treatment and, at the same time, serving as the ultimate authority from which theory and technique may be derived, must now be further concretized. It is inadequate in that a rigorously theoretical way of arguing is replaced by narrative structures – the 'inner' perspectives of a literary text – but these narrative structures have to be brought into the service of the theory. Because the separate fragments cannot be properly linked together, a field of tensions arises: the reader must supply the missing connections himself in his endeavours to build consistency or, in Freud's words, the reader must 'put together' the various perspectives 'into a living whole'. The persuasive power and didactic value that characterize Freud's case histories thus result from the paradox that the specific structure of the text – the dubious way in which a theoretically cogent deduction of axioms and claims from philosophical concepts is replaced by narrative technique – calls for the reader's active participation in the constitution of meaning: in order to effect an undisturbed and smooth reading process, the reader must complement the text. The connections made between the divergent 'inner' perspectives are products of the reader and not of the text. The reader, however, will always find his own mental conjectures plausible, probably even more so than the most rigorous of theoretical deductions supplied by a text.

Freud's later case histories display the pattern of complicated literary plots, taking into account on the one hand the specific eventfulness of psychoanalytic treatment which they highlight, and on the other hand meeting the basic human need for concord fictions. Moreover, by employing Iser's theory of aesthetic response, I could show that the very splintering of the data into five thematic perspectives which, again, point to three different fields of reference calls for an active involvement on the part of the recipient. Instead of being offered a cogent deduction of philosophical propositions (theoretically sound deductions are the main characteristics of any form of theoretical discourse), the reader has to come up with connections of his own. The ways in which he fills the gaps between the inner perspectives of the text are not arbitrary, but controlled by the textual environment, by other perspectives which refer to the same material (the contingencies involved in psychoanalytic treatment).

However, these two aspects do not in themselves suffice to justify my hypothesis that the theoretical type of psychopathography assimilates literary discourse and, in doing so, is subliminally converted into literary discourse. The one characteristic whereby literary discourse is singled out from any other form of discourse is a certain amount of self-reflexivity, an incessant attempt to unveil its own literary strategies by centring attention on the fact that whatever is depicted is only fictional and has no truth-value whatsoever. Nowadays, moreover, the notion that anything can actually be represented by language is considered an illusion, and consequently any explanations offered by narrative discourse are automatically suspected of lacking validity. Freud is indebted to the traditions of literary modernism in that he not only draws attention in his case histories to the problems involved in conveying the contingencies of psychoanalytic treatment in written form, but also questions their inherent claim to validity.

Case histories are characterized by the fact that they have to convey a chain of significant signs stretching from a specific set of symptoms to an experience which caused them. This chain of significant signs contains a temporal dimension. The eventfulness of psychoanalytic treatment, the tensions between space and time, are – in the written record of case histories, as in the psychoanalyst's interpretations – transformed into concord fictions. The structure underlying all case histories, therefore, is the same as that of conventional historiography, which postulates that our present society can be explained only by digging out and understanding the origins from which it has developed.

In the Wolf-Man analysis, a primal scene[25] with which the Wolf-Man was confronted as a child of 18 months seems to constitute the ultimate origin of all his conflicts and symptoms, that *beginning* whereby the chain of significant signs and that *end* whereby the symptoms can – apparently – be explained. However, as soon as Freud has revealed this origin in his case history, he begins to question the origin's status as an event which actually, historically, *did* take place. In a postscript added in 1918 (he had originally written the case history in 1914–15, when the First World War compelled him to interrupt his treatment of the Wolf-Man), Freud discusses the question of whether the Wolf-Man did observe a primal scene or whether he merely phantasized it:

> I did not require the contributions of Adler or Jung to induce me to consider the matter with a critical eye, and to bear in mind the possibility that what analysis puts forward as being forgotten experiences of childhood (and of an improbably early childhood) may . . . be based upon phantasies created on occasions occurring later in life. According to this view, wherever we seemed in analyses to see traces of the after-effects of an infantile impression of the kind

in question, we should rather have to assume that we were faced by the manifestation of some constitutional factor or of some disposition that had been phylogenetically maintained . . . I was the first . . . to recognize both the part played by phantasies in symptom-formation and also the 'retrospective phantasying' of late impressions into childhood and their sexualization after the event . . . If, in spite of this, I have held to the more difficult and more improbable view, it has been as a result of arguments such as are forced upon the investigator by the case described in these pages or by any other infantile neurosis – arguments which I once again lay before my readers for their decision.[26]

In the final resort, Freud here postulates a *phantasy* rather than an *event* as the more probable. The origin of this phantasy is a 'phylogenetically maintained disposition'. That disposition, however, carries the phantasy in question well beyond the unconscious: at least, beyond Freud's concept of an unconscious. According to Freud, the unconscious is an entity which consists of repressed mental images, is dominated by the structures, mechanisms and laws of the primary process,[27] and defies conscious control. In fervent opposition to Freud's concept of an unconscious, C.G. Jung postulated a collective unconscious, farther removed from the conscious ego than the Freudian unconscious, and containing archetypes and archetypal structures. Jung's collective unconscious is shared by and accessible to all humanity. The collective unconscious includes supra-individual, primeval human experience which, according to Jung, fosters our creativity.[28]

At a crucial point in his theoretical argument, Freud replaces an event by a phantasy, by a figment of the imagination, and then displaces it even farther by associating it with a collective unconscious. Case histories – and here again we have a parallel to mediating texts – are based on authenticity, on the validity of evidence deducted from actual life, from the patient's life story as well as from the eventfulness and contingencies inherent in the psychoanalytic venture as shared by analyst and patient. However, if therapeutic treatment can be captured only in literary discourse and, in addition, if the patient's life story is grounded in phantasies, then a considerable amount of mingling of the authentic with the imaginary is at work in case histories. This does not seem to bother Freud; he claims that both psychoanalytic treatments and the written accounts of them, the case histories, maintain their validity no matter whether an imaginary entity or an actual event is taken as the vantage point. While this shift may be considered of minor relevance to both therapeutic treatment and narrative technique, Freud is replacing – and this is of vital importance – one form of concord fiction (characterized by

an integration of time with the spatial structure of origin/chain of significant signs/symptoms) by another in which the origin is even farther
displaced to many other chains of significant signs (the contents of a
collective unconscious).

Considered in the light of his final statement, Freud is telling two structurally different stories. It is up to the reader to decide which version, in
retrospect, he thinks is correct: the first adopts the narrative technique
and the intentionality of conventional historiography (ends are consonant with origins), whereas the second highlights the problematic status
of all narrative discourse: once language is conceived of as a system of
interfering signs which are deprived of their capability to denote but only
connote ever more signs (whole chains of signs, leading up to ever more
stories), then the question of origins is replaced by the concept of a multiple intertextual referentiality which is potentially endless.

However, if the assumed *origin* of a symptom is an imaginary entity
implying further chains of significant signs, then no *end* in consonance
with this imaginary origin can be projected, even by reconstructing the
chains of association on which therapeutic treatment is based (they themselves are only phantasy products). The Wolf-Man's character profile –
any character is usually seen as the sum of certain prominent and stable
character structures – is thus regarded as being essentially de-centred.
Corresponding to this is the fact that the unconscious itself is an entity
lacking a temporal dimension. Only through integrating a spatially
structured chain of significant signs with the temporal dimensions of a
psychoanalytic treatment can it ever acquire meaning and significance.
However, for the very reason that the unconscious lacks temporal structures, all psychoanalysis is potentially unlimited, 'end-less'.[29] Freud's concept of the subject as de-centred is, in its turn, characteristic of the concept
of the subject prevalent in the philosophic traditions of poststructuralism,
traditions which did not develop until the middle of the twentieth
century.[30]

Freud's case histories interpolate narrative techniques, and at the same
time they reveal that stories connote either further stories or entities which
lack temporal structures (the individual and/or the collective unconscious). The genre of 'case history' as a form of discourse both elaborating
on and containing the concept of origin/chain of significant signs/
symptoms is an invention of Freud's; he himself, however, innovated and
subsequently subverted the genre to such an extent that eventually he
even dismantled its very basis. Case histories – like the psychoanalytic
interpretations upon which both treatment and written accounts of it
depend – are stripped of their ideological components and shown to be
essentially imaginary in nature.

Although nowadays all acts of narration – and especially their inherent claim to veracity – are subject to subversion, with Freud himself happily perpetuating (or rather anticipating) that tradition, nevertheless, in case histories to narrate is an imperative. As the relation between cause and effect, between beginning and end, is lacking, the story acquires its significance only because it is told and therefore endowed with a 'meaningful' structure. Kermode writes (again referring to literary fictions): 'They are not subject, like hypotheses, to proof or disconfirmation, only, if they come to lose their operational effectiveness, to neglect.'[31] The function of the theoretical type of psychopathography, its 'operational effectiveness', consists, despite – or perhaps because of – all the self-referentiality in its discourse, in its didactic dimension. Didactics, however, depend on having a reliable, meaningful and structured universe at their disposal – even if only in the form of a text.

Having discussed both the conventions of psychoanalytic case histories and those far-reaching innovations that Freud himself effected within the paradigm he had founded, I shall examine the way in which the theoretical type of psychopathography has been even further modified by Freud's successors.

When writing about her therapeutic technique, Fromm-Reichmann is confronted with all those problems of discourse mentioned above. In addition, she was not treating neurotic structures, like Freud, but psychotic phenomena, which complicates her procedures: the subjective dimensions of counter-transference – on which the therapeutic treatment of psychosis is based – makes it very difficult to deduce her therapeutic technique in a cogent and comprehensive way from metapsychology. My hypothesis is that psychoanalysts who take psychoses and the question of their amenability to treatment as a subject of theoretical investigations will be forced to change the conventions of the genre case histories by coming up with yet further literary innovations.

Since a new subject area, i.e. the terms of a psychoanalytic treatment of *psychosis* (as opposed to psychoanalytically orientated psychotherapy or classic Freudian psychoanalysis), will be discussed in the following pages, I shall begin by introducing some of the modalities of such a treatment.

### The treatment of psychosis, a new development in Freudian psychoanalysis

Every psychoanalytically orientated psychotherapy is based on a relationship between therapist and patient, exemplary as well as imaginary, in which old and new forms of relationship are re-enacted or invented. Not only the relationship between psychoanalyst and patient, but also the passage of time (parallel to that passage of time in the patient's actual life extending from the origin of his symptoms to the phase when his mental illness was finally surfacing) plays a decisive role in treatment: initial anxiety is dissipated and emotional insights can be assimilated *in time*. Psychotherapeutic technique consists of both elements, of the therapist's part in an exemplary (if only imaginary) human relationship as well as in his active, structuring interventions into the contingent passage of time during treatment.

The 'one and only' psychoanalytic technique does not exist. It might be possible to invent or construct it, if therapeutic techniques could be comprehensively derived from metapsychology. But not even Freud himself was able to do that. His own writings bear witness that he always made a clinical discovery *first*, and *then* sought to integrate it into the body of his already existing theories, often being obliged to modify them considerably in the process. (This is the reason why Freudian psychoanalysis contains six different and equally valid concepts of the human psyche, which can be employed either separately or in various combinations, according to the specific nature of the phenomenon in question.) Metapsychology has always drawn upon psychoanalytic technique, and not vice versa.

Another reason why it is impossible to derive any therapeutic technique directly and in unmitigated form from metapsychology is that the psychoanalyst intervenes in the psychoanalytic process through the weight of his personality, by means of his subjectivity. The psychoanalyst himself, however, is subject to repercussions from his unconscious; his subjectivity cannot be moulded into a rigid and sterile mechanism for churning out the required interventions and psychoanalytic interpretations: no psychoanalyst will ever be able to convert theory into technique in a flawless, mechanical manner. The concepts of psychoanalytic technique serve only as guidelines; they are mere crutches, a system of coordinates whereby the psychoanalyst can keep his own conflicting impulses under control. Therefore, every intervention by the psychoanalyst which is motivated by the demands of psychoanalytic technique alone might be just an acting out of his defence mechanisms. Fritz Morgenthaler, in his book *Technik: Zur Dialektik der psychoanalytischen Praxis* (Frankfurt, 1978), argues that owing to the uniqueness of every encounter between the psychoanalyst and his patient, psychoanalytic technique cannot be conceptualized – and thus *cannot be learned*. (Its philosophical foundations, on the other hand, *can*.) Elements of ambiguity, contradiction and dissatisfaction play a role in all human interaction, including psychoanalytic treatment. The fact that through the encounter of two people a subjective component enters into the psychoanalytic process is *one* of the reasons for the problem of communication which arises whenever therapeutic technique is to be conveyed in the form of case histories.

Although there has never been anything like a 'one and only' psychoanalytic technique, it is obvious that Freud's successors have split into two divergent schools of technique. They are usually referred to as the school of 'classic technique' and the school of 'corrective emotional experience'.[32] Classic technique aims at bringing about rational insights and works deductively, taking ego-psychology as its frame of reference. It can be labelled a 'paternalistic therapy of reason'.[33] The school of corrective emotional experience, on the other hand, works inductively, on the basis of rather speculative theories about a phase of human development before language acquisition (which means before the structuring of the psyche into different functions, like those of id, ego and super-ego), and can be conceived of as a 'therapy of maternal love'.[34]

If the origin of psychopathological disorders lies in phases of human development which precede language acquisition and ego-differentiation, then the therapeutic treatment of such disorders must enable the patient to regress to phases of symbiotic fusion or psychotic dissolution. Therapeutic interventions cannot work on the repressed, on unconscious conflicts – rational insights and understanding are required to mediate and ultimately integrate those – but only on the defect. In his therapeutic relationship with the psychoanalyst, the aim is for the patient to have an emotional experience which he was denied in his relationship with his mother, and thus to correct his negative experiences. This requires an attitude in the psychoanalyst which differs radically from that of the technique invented by Freud: Freud holds that since transference occurs almost automatically, the psychoanalyst can refrain from active participation and limit his role to that of an interested observer. In the technique of corrective emotional experience, on the other hand, transference becomes possible only as a reaction to intensive efforts made by the psychoanalyst on the patient's behalf. In the course of the therapy, the psychoanalyst finds himself forced to involve himself in the psychotic process and, in order to do that, to distance himself from his own psychic structures. This leads to a fundamentally different role of counter-transference in treatment: where it is a purely diagnostic instrument in the classic technique, here it is a prerequisite of therapy, and consequently it must precede any transference situation. Interpretations too acquire a different status: where Freud wanted his patients to gain insight into their unconscious defence mechanisms by being confronted with his interpretations, in a therapy which aims at a corrective emotional experience interpretations are seen to be superfluous if not actually destructive.

Fromm-Reichmann belongs to the school of corrective emotional experience. Her method of treatment is based almost exclusively on empathy, which she uses as a means of restoring the early mother–child relationship. Empathy can be allocated a specific function in the

therapeutic context described above, but it cannot be conclusively conceptualized (as opposed to Freud's main therapeutic strategy, his interpretations of his patients' resistance, which can be conceptualized), since
empathy is *wholly subjective* by nature and inherent in the therapist's
counter-transference. This factor makes it problematic to document
therapeutic technique in case histories.

Theoretically speaking, counter-transference is closely linked to transference, that is, to the repetition of infantile patterns of relationship with
the psychoanalyst. In schizophrenics, transference is marked by a specific
ambivalence: anxiety, suspicion and hostile impulses towards the therapist clash with an acute sense of becoming rather dependent on his attention. The patient's ambivalent transference, the high degree of anxiety he
feels during intensive uncovering treatment, and the long phases of stag-
nation during which his treatment seems to get nowhere, may in their turn
trigger off a negative counter-transference in the therapist.

In the terminology of classic psychoanalysis, counter-transference is
conceived of as the psychoanalyst's unconscious reaction to his patient's
transference; Fromm-Reichmann argues, instead, for a totalistic, all-
encompassing notion of counter-transference: she subsumes all the
psychoanalyst's feelings and attitudes towards his patient under this one
concept. In her theory of therapeutic treatment, it is counter-transference
which is highly ambivalent. On the one hand, she uses counter-
transference as an effective tool for registering and understanding her
patients' transference (in this respect her handling of counter-transference
is close to Freud's); on the other hand, however, counter-transference for
Fromm-Reichmann is the very source of energy that stimulates, conditions and regulates the empathy she needs for treating her psychotic
patients: 'One way of looking at a psychiatrist's intuitive awareness is to
see it as a function of his well-recognized countertransference experiences
with his patient. It should, however, be understood that counter-
transference experiences are . . . intuitive processes [and] potentially
limitless.'[35] As Fromm-Reichmann aims at encountering her patients while
they regress deeply into undifferentiation, into stages before language
acquisition, her concept of treatment is based on empathy and on
highly ambivalent transference and counter-transference reactions. While
all-encompassing ambivalence is of fundamental importance for the
progress of Fromm-Reichmann's therapeutic treatment, it defies
conceptualization.

All therapy is based on human interaction with all its vicissitudes. In
Fromm-Reichmann's concept of therapy, however, further and more
virulent dimensions of subjectivity come into play, for the very reason
that in her notion of treatment, transference and counter-transference
originate in an interpersonal relationship that is highly symbiotic. How,

then, can these highly complex processes be described and conveyed in the theoretical type of psychopathography as developed by Freud?

### Frieda Fromm-Reichmann's case histories

In three essays, Fromm-Reichmann mentions Greenberg's psychotherapy; these are: 'Some Aspects of Psychoanalytic Psychotherapy with Schizophrenics' (1952), 'Psychotherapy of Schizophrenia' (1954) and 'Basic Problems in the Psychotherapy of Schizophrenia' (1958). She six times interpolates passages dealing with Greenberg's therapy into her theoretical discourse.[36] Her fragmented narratives convey the image of a patient who enters into an essentially negative transference relationship with her therapist, in analogy to the difficult relationship she had with her parents in early childhood. (In a negative transference relationship, the unconscious wishes directed to the psychoanalyst carry less impact than the patient's provocative and obnoxious behaviour which is marked by suspicion, rejection, hatred etc.) As a result of Greenberg's negative feelings, the therapeutic treatment is severely impeded, and the patient will not give up her manifest symptoms (suicide attempts, burning and pulling off pieces of her skin). During therapeutic sessions, she frequently lapses into phases marked by hallucinations and delusions (i.e. acute psychotic attacks), which almost entirely defy therapeutic intervention and make admission to hospital seem inevitable. In the course of the treatment, more and more events from the patient's childhood, dating back to ever earlier periods in her life, are revealed and discussed, until the uncovering treatment finally discloses the meaning of her symptoms. Subsequently, they are worked through, and the patient's acute anxiety can be dissipated to such an extent that she is discharged first from the psychiatric hospital and later from her therapeutic treatment in a relatively stable condition.

In Fromm-Reichmann's case histories, as in Freud's, the documentation of the conversation which takes place during therapy does not in itself suffice to convey what psychoanalytic treatment is all about; rather, an integration of expanding and structuring factors, of spatial and temporal structures, has to be achieved. Where Freud invented and elaborated on an intricate system of multi-layered and interacting perspectives, Fromm-Reichmann, at least in her writing, reduces the apparent multi-dimensional nature of treatment to mere monocausal connections.

First and foremost, this is achieved by simply juxtaposing two different forms of discourse, their difference being signalled by a contrast in typefaces:

> Now, to illustrate the therapeutic approach in terms of scrutiny along the lines of the patient's anxiety, its various manifestations,

and her defenses against it, as I have outlined it in this and previous papers:

*A patient shouted at the psychiatrist during their [sic] first visit, 'I know what you will do now! You'll take my gut-pains, and my trance, and my withdrawal states away from me! And where will I be then?' The psychiatrist first asked for a description of the three pathological states, the loss of which the patient allegedly feared. The patient's answer made it possible for the psychiatrist to demonstrate to her the attempt at escaping anxiety, which all three of the states had in common. Subsequently, her anxiety regarding the psychiatrist's role as a foe rather than as a co-worker was labeled as such, and the historical roots for this interpersonal attitude and expectation could be scrutinized. After that the patient was told that her symptoms would not be taken away from her but that, in all likelihood, she herself would wish to dispose of them when she learned to understand enough about her anxiety to make it decrease. Also the patient's attention was drawn to the fact that she had made her symptoms known immediately to the psychiatrist. It was suggested that this seemed to indicate that, perhaps without realizing it, she was just as desirous of losing her symptoms as she was anxious, within her awareness, at the prospect of being deprived of them. Thus psychiatrist and patient were in the middle of a therapeutic discussion of various aspects of the patient's anxiety right at the beginning of her treatment.*

Later on, the treatment history of this patient was characterized by a pattern of relapsing into disturbed states of withdrawal and self-mutilation and of resorting to painful hallucinations and delusions which she had previously relinquished. This occurred whenever another new symptom was resolved or whenever she gave away another telling secret from her private world. The hostility against the analyst and the family and the anxiety aroused by this hostility could be seen by the patient, and its repetitive connection with previous similar situations in camp, school, and family could be investigated.[37]

The interpolated passage of text, which refers to Greenberg's treatment, is merely a summary of the therapy, and a rather abstract one at that. Abstractions dominate every summary (and all forms of theoretical discourse). In the passage quoted above, even the narrative perspective is tainted by abstractions: an 'omniscient narrator' is reporting in a distanced manner, and without reference to the therapist's intensive personal participation in the eventfulness of the therapy described; countertransference phenomena are not even mentioned. Another distancing factor consists in the fact that Fromm-Reichmann is writing about several different patients in one and the same essay; the unique nature of the encounter between therapist and patient is not taken into account, but concealed by the notion that people, therapeutic situations and relationships are interchangeable at will. Moreover, the important chain of significant signs running between symptom and origin is not even mentioned. A remark such as 'The patient's answer made it possible for the psychiatrist to demonstrate to her the attempt at escaping anxiety' does not convey the chain of associations leading up to this answer, nor does it indicate what associations it consisted in. The course of time necessary for the gaps and links in a spatially structured chain of significant signs to surface is not documented: no integration of spatial and temporal structures by means of concord fictions takes place. Concord fictions are replaced by a false harmony, brought about by the illusion that there actually is a linear and monocausal consonance between the symptoms and their origins.

In addition, the theoretical frames of reference for the narrative fragments do not lie in realms beyond the discourse in question, but are contained in it. They form their intratextual environment. There is a clear distinction between those elements which are necessary for the discussion of theory and technique, and the narrative elements. The story merely serves to introduce the theoretical notions *yet again*, even if in another form of discourse. Different typefaces guarantee that both passages dealing with identical material, but in different forms of discourse, will be adequately processed. Every form of discourse is characterized by the fact that it gives rise to and carries expectations as to its own good continuation. These expectations are thwarted. However, subverting expectations does not automatically lead to literary innovation. Moreover, the clash of two forms of discourse, the theoretical and the narrative, is now an established convention of the genre 'case history' signalling that the same material is discussed *twice*. The function of this device is to foster and enhance the didacticism inherent in the genre. Whenever any material is presented in two consecutive forms of discourse, persuasive power is engendered, although – arguing with Iser's theory of aesthetic response – this persuasiveness does not display the same intensity as that of Freud's case histories, because it is not effected by the reader's active participation in the reading process. Fromm-Reichmann's persuasions are *over*-powering to her readers, while the textual strategies in Freud's discourse demand the reader's lively imagination to work on processing the text and accepting its argument.

Although Fromm-Reichmann discusses material which is not amenable to verbalization, her texts display – paradoxically – an *over*-fulfilment of the pattern developed by Freud for the genre 'case history', instead of subverting the paradigm by literary innovations. Neither does her discourse take into account our anthropological need for complex concord fictions, nor contain that dynamic momentum which is active in every set genre pattern in literature, urging it to open up and change.

Mediating texts, as I conceptualized them in chapter 2, also draw upon set literary schemata (the patterns of the eighteenth-century novel). Therefore, they too could be classified by the notion that they over-fulfil a paradigm. However, there is no such thing as *the* eighteenth-century novel, any more than there is any such thing as the 'one and only' psychoanalytic technique. When we speak of 'the eighteenth-century novel', we imply and project a theoretical construct, a collection of several formal features. As compared with the complexity inherent in every individual eighteenth-century novel, this abstract entity is bound to look like an impoverishment if not actually a falsification. It is upon such a construct – rather than on the novels themselves – that mediating texts draw. Within this genre, the function of over-fulfilling a literary paradigm is to conceal the literariness of the text in question, and to initiate a reading process which has a stabilizing effect. In Fromm-Reichmann, the over-fulfilment seems to have a similar function: her *over*-powering discourse is certainly stabilizing (if not boring).

Case histories contain literary strategies due to their being a form of narrative discourse; in Fromm-Reichmann's case histories, however, even the narrative fragments are marked by abstractions – which themselves are a component of all theoretical forms of discourse – rather than by literary strategies and schemata. Her texts assimilate the sterile abstractions of theory rather than the liveliness of literature. No reference is ever made to the problem of how to verbalize realms of experience which defy interpersonal communication, whereas Freud again and again discusses the possibilities and the limitations of conveying the intricacies of a psychoanalytic treatment through writing. In Fromm-Reichman's over-fulfilment of the paradigm, a subversion of the genre is unthinkable, for not only (as in mediating texts) is the literariness of her texts veiled, so is that fictional element characteristic of both case histories and analytic interpretations. As soon as fictions no longer advertise the fact that they are fictions, they run the risk of becoming fixed in dogmatism; they easily degenerate into myths, a phenomenon which Kermode has analysed:

> We have to distinguish between myths and fictions. Fictions can degenerate into myths whenever they are not consciously held to be fictive . . . Myth operates within the diagrams of ritual, which presupposes total and adequate explanations of things as they are and were; it is a sequence of radically unchangeable gestures. Fictions are for finding things out, and they change as the needs of

sense-making change. Myths are the agents of stability, fictions the agents of change. Myths call for absolute, fictions for conditional assent.[38]

The fact that Fromm-Reichmann transforms the genre case history so that it presupposes 'total and adequate explanations of things as they are' has consequences for the reader's responses to her texts. The monocausal connections within a stable frame of reference presented by her texts do not call on the reader to complement the text, to supply missing links by means of mental projections. Like every theoretical text, this case history (despite the literariness inherent in the genre) exclusively activates the intellectual faculties of the reader, who can choose only between accepting or rejecting the material presented as true or false; he is allowed no wider range of reactions.

The truth-value of representation in fictional texts is rather precarious, and is becoming increasingly so in our times. Freud takes this phenomenon into account. Fromm-Reichmann's writings, on the other hand, have a dogmatic effect precisely because they conceal their fictional elements, and subliminally degenerate into myth. (This danger is at least potentially present in all case histories.) Here again, we have a parallel to the literary type of mediating text: new series of texts can come into being only when the dynamic factor inherent in all literary genres, their openness to formal and/or thematic innovation, is exploited, whereas the imitative type of mediating text, a truly degenerative form, restricts itself to repeating the once successful pattern of the literary type of mediating text again and again, and with no apparent variation.

Case histories are first and foremost a didactic genre. They offer a theoretical argument, and aim at initiating a reading process that is predominantly rational. This is the aspect that links them to the theoretical type of mediating text. I have therefore classified psychoanalytic case histories as the theoretical type of psychopathography. The contingencies involved in psychotherapeutic treatment move both the treatments and the written accounts of them into realms beyond the margins of discourse. As for my initial hypothesis that a theoretical form of discourse – when confronted with a problem of communication – will assimilate literary strategies and thereby approach the status of a narrative, it has been possible to confirm it, but with a modification. Paradoxically, only those case histories which are firmly rooted in the tradition of literary modernism carry out their didactic intention of convincing their readers by their arguments; they subvert their own paradigm, incorporate a dynamic openness and prestructure a reading process during which the reader's active involvement in processing the text forces him to come up with a multitude of mental images of his own. These mental images fill in gaps in the theoretical argument, and are subsequently substituted for any missing theoretical deductions, thereby making the argument more convincing (no reader will readily consider his own mental conjectures false). However, as soon as the status of case histories as fictions, and concord fictions at that, is obscured and they fail to display a certain amount of self-reflexivity by advertising the fact that they contain fictional elements, then dogmatic rigidity is at hand.

# 5

# The imitative type of psychopathography

Hannah Green's novel *I Never Promised You a Rose Garden* (New York, 1964)[1] occupies an interesting position within the psychopathography genre: like the literary type of psychopathography, this novel attempts to depict a psychotic dissolution of personality. Moreover, the novel incorporates fragments of the same therapy described in Fromm-Reichmann's writings, which belong to the theoretical type of psychopathography. Thus, the novel is afflicted by problems similar to those of the case histories: how to integrate antagonistic forces, and at the same time convey their impact and destructiveness. A case history (which is a didactic genre aiming to convey information about therapeutic technique) lays emphasis on the therapist's structuring interventions and interpretations. A narrative from the patient's viewpoint, however, will have to take into account the liveliness and vicissitudes of therapeutic treatment and of the psychotic attacks leading up to it, that is to say, their subjective, expanding factors. So how can a patient tell the story of his or her own psychoanalytic treatment?

As every psychoanalysis is of its nature closely linked to the analysand's life story, one might at first expect such an account to be a sub-genre of autobiography. However, that would entail replacing the exemplum of a life story by the exemplum of intrapersonal changes initiated by psychoanalysis. A structural scheme like 'mental suffering/ intrapersonal changes/better life' would also mean that a therapy could be recorded only after it was completed, thus allowing a field of tension to arise between a more mature ego telling the story – from a considerable distance in time – of his or her intrapersonal changes and the subsequent positive influence those changes brought to bear in later life. This, however, is precisely the formula that is rejected in both Erlenberger's and Lessing's novels: this relatively rigid scheme does not lend itself to communicating the openness and expansion of psychotic attacks and psychotherapeutic treatment. At best, such a formula can be turned into propaganda for psychoanalytic treatment, because it could enhance the illusion that it might be possible to lead a subjectively more satisfactory life. Employing this structural pattern would certainly bring any depiction of the vicissitudes inherent in psychoanalytic treatment close to becoming a mediating text.

As I have already mentioned,[2] publications about the writer's own psychoanalysis are relatively rare. Accounts of training analyses react to the problem of discourse outlined above by concentrating on therapeutic technique (and thus, like the case histories, on the structuring elements inherent in psychoanalytic treatment). Published accounts of training analyses assimilate the textual strategies of case histories, and thereby approach the theoretical type of psychopathography. The reason why there are so few accounts of psychoanalyses whose objective is the treatment of mental illness, rather than the training of psychoanalysts, is obviously that they lack a textual paradigm. Case histories cannot function as a paradigm. Consequently, every single account of a psychoanalysis, like every individual literary type of psychopathography, must confront and react in its own idiosyncratic way to the problem of exactly how to tell the story of one's own therapy. At this point one might raise the objection that the literary type of psychopathography has no paradigm at its disposal either, and yet many such texts are being published at present. Obviously, they feed on some undercurrent of modern society: the literary type of psychopathography plays to a certain extent with the collective fear that society's all-encompassing concern with radical individuality might tip over into pathological dimensions whereas the fascination emanating from the arcane mysteries of psychoanalysis does not seem to stir up collective phantasies – at least, not at present.

The title of Green's novel indicates that its author was in therapy with Fromm-Reichmann.[3] Her manifest symptoms (burning and pulling off pieces of skin) and her specific system of delusions (a counter-reality, an alternative world with a language of its own)[4] also point to the fact that the therapy referred to is the same in both cases.[5] *I Never Promised You a Rose Garden* is obviously based on its author's personal experience of psychotic phenomena and their therapeutic treatment. However, this fact is not revealed in the text. Although the specific events described, the acute psychotic attacks and the psychotherapy, would seem to lend themselves to a first-person narration (because of the subjective, expanding elements involved), the novel is written in the third person. An omniscient narrator introduces all the minor characters who appear in the novel and, even less plausibly, offers an inner perspective on their personalities. This, however, is not the only conventional strategy of representation in the novel. All the dramatic elements that move the plot are brought into play as early as the exposition: the bewildered parents, the understanding and empathizing woman doctor, the sensitive protagonist, her fascinating and ambivalently charged world of delusions and the setting (a psychiatric hospital). There is even a conventional sub-plot: before the happy ending can occur (the dissolution of the symptoms and the protagonist's subsequent reintegration into society), her parents have to undergo a kind of 'inverted therapy' in which they not only accept their daughter's psychopathology but also learn to stand up for it, to themselves and to others. Time is linear. The form of the text is entirely drawn from the pattern of literary strategies which dominate schematic literature.

The problem of how to convey psychotic phenomena in literary discourse – the very problem whereby the text can be classified as a psychopathography – is tackled by depicting the autistically closed phantasy world in which Deborah, the protagonist, finds herself imprisoned with the conventional literary device of a 'story within a story'.[6] Her symptoms take the form of a largely *conscious* system of defence mechanisms; she uses them to shut herself off from her environment, so that both communication and therapy must seem impossible. The story of the therapeutic treatment is presented as a battle for the protagonist's phantasy world, a phantasy world which she invests with an abundance of conflicting emotions. It is this battle that propels the plot and builds up suspense as to its outcome. However, the imaginary world does not act as an irritant on the reader's responses to the novel, since passages in which the protagonist's phantasies are described are always printed in italics, so that the typeface itself is turned into a signal which allows for an easy integration of these narrative passages into the hierarchy of textual perspectives.

Apart from a certain suspense, no emotions are aroused in the reader, whereas in the novel anxiety is frequently described: ' "All right – you'll ask me questions and I'll answer them – you'll clear up my 'symptoms' and send me home . . . *and what will I have then?*" The doctor said quietly, "If you did not really want to give them up, you wouldn't tell me." A rope of fear pulled its noose about Deborah.'[7] In this passage, anxiety is metaphorically depicated as 'a rope of fear'. The metaphor, however, is not expressed by the protagonist (who is overcome by the very feeling to which the metaphor refers) but by the omniscient narrator. The rather authoritarian way of narrating thus reaffirms its total control over all events, while at the same time it distances the reader from the subjective and oppressive dimensions of the anxiety in question. And the metaphor itself is merely a cliché.

The violent, expanding elements in both psychotic personality dissolutions and therapeutic processes are labelled and controlled by a distant narrative agency which, in turn, effects aesthetic distance: the protagonist's fragile contacts with other patients, her interpersonal relationships, the therapeutic treatment and her committal to the psychiatric hospital are merely *said to be* highly charged with anxiety. Naming anxiety by stating that psychopathological material is charged with that feeling, however, does not allow for its aesthetic communication.

The reader's role contained in the text is comparable with that in a detective novel, with the struggle for the protagonist's renunciation of her phantasy world providing a kind of suspense similar to the hunting down of the murderer. The reader's response is characterized (as in the imitative type of mediating text) by contemplation (if not by boredom).

Aesthetic distance results from the fact that the events in the novel are not related by, say, a lyrical 'I' (as in *Der Hunger nach Wahnsinn* and, at least in part, in *The Golden Notebook*), but by an omniscient narrator; aesthetic distance is an important factor in controlling the reader's response. No authoritarian and distancing narrative agency will ever be able to capture the contingencies involved in a writing process which – through actively facing the impact of self-reflexivity inherent in all writing processes – gives rise to fundamental personality changes.[8] The conventionally told story does not communicate the eventfulness of emotional progress; it depicts situations occurring along a way that has already been clearly marked out, with its beginning and ending as well as its carefully chosen intermediate steps: *I Never Promised You a Rose Garden* represents arrested transitional stages, not a process. All this adds up to evoking in the reader the impression of stasis. The novel's clear structure of hierarchically arranged textual strategies is rather static in itself. A prevalent sense of stasis, however, is something totally alien to the dynamics involved in both psychotic attacks and the process of therapeutic treatment.

The imitative type of psychopathography draws upon and takes over the textual strategies and perspectives of both the literary type of psychopathography and schematic literary genres, and employs them in a trite way. Anxiety is merely named, described on a thematic level, but is never contained in the textual strategies, and therefore can be no part of the aesthetic response. *I Never Promised You a Rose Garden* certainly does not offer a satisfactory answer to the question 'How can someone tell the story of his or her own analysis?' A paradigm for such a type of text has yet to be constructed. It calls for two simultaneous yet divergent narrative agencies: to allow for the twofold structure of therapeutic processes which are essentially based on dialogue (on expanding and structuring elements, progressive and regressive time axes, the exchanges between a self and a second person), another, alien and alienating speech would have to be interpolated into the narrator's own, submerged into it, yet surfacing at odd times with momentum. Therapies and the written accounts of them are of their nature de-centred and endless. No omniscient narrator employing an authoritarian, explanatory narrative will ever be able to communicate their anatagonistic and dynamic elements. Only by recapturing in writing the analysand's endless utterances (which are incomplete, but not 'false'), their intertwining chains of significant signs, and contrasting them with the psychoanalyst's hermeneutic efforts as well as with the inadequacies inherent in them, would it be possible to project an eventfulness into fixed textual structures while simultaneously subverting or even negating them. Only thus might a reader be convinced – and to carry conviction is the aim of all narrative processes, even those which (like Freud's case histories) are constantly obliged to negate their fictional status because of the precarious mode of existence of the phenomena they recount.

# 6

## The virtual dimension of psychopathographies

Psychopathographies comprise a quantity of apparently quite different texts: traditional pathographies (Freud's case histories) as well as those texts about psychoses which, as a phenomenon of contemporary literature, have not yet had the critical attention they deserve. In this book, I started out by *hypothetically* defining psychopathographies by two criteria, one of content and one of aesthetic response. Psychopathographies thematize psychotic personality dissolutions and/or psychotherapies, and are thus obliged to grapple with phenomena beyond the margins of discourse. The way in which a psychopathography translates psychotic phenomena into linguistic structures determines, in turn, the extent to which such a borderline situation can be conveyed, and even experienced, in the reading process.

In chapters 3–5, I discussed the textual strategies entering into and, in their sum, making up the communicatory situation in the literary, theoretical and imitative types of psychopathography. I showed that while those types of psychopathography able to produce interesting responses do supply the reader with directions as to how he should concretize their subject area during the reading process, they do not express it in so many words. A naive spelling out, on the other hand, is more typical of the imitative type of psychopathography and of certain degenerative forms of the theoretical type, as my analysis of Fromm-Reichmann's writings indicates.

However, the communicatory situation between text and reader is not *exclusively* effected by formal textual strategies. The reader takes an active part in the reading process in so far as he does not simply concretize the strata of formal structures written into the text, but also brings phantasies of his own to bear. These phantasies are to some extent pre-structured and controlled by formal perspectives, but are not entirely contained in them. Extra-textual components influence the reading process too.

I will call these extra-textual components the *virtual dimension* of psychopathographies: virtual in that, although this dimension is necessary for the communication of the subject area in question – where it is lacking, as in the imitative type of text (and the degenerative theoretical type), no interesting responses occur – it seems impossible to pin it down to or identify it with any definite position in the text.

Psychoses and the therapeutic treatment of psychoses are areas of experience which implode our ordinary frames of reference for understanding and interpreting our world. Talking about such phenomena in a literary or a theoretical text in itself suffices to instigate phantasies which are founded in the reader's personal, subjective dispositions, which are free-floating and expansive, and which defy systematization (unless one wants to apply the rather dubious category of classification according to the 'average breadth of association' to which topics give rise).

The virtual dimension of psychopathographies, however, is not altogether expansive; there are factors which do exert a certain control over it. Here, as always, the constricting factors can be more easily grasped than the expanding tendencies. In the case of the theoretical type of text, calls are made on the rational and/or emotional faculties of the recipient; in the case of the literary type of text, on his literary competence resulting from his knowledge of mediating texts, i.e. a learned capacity.

The theoretical type of psychopathography is a didactic genre. Case histories and accounts of therapies want to convince their readers of their arguments; their most prominent function is their operational effectiveness. They aim to make certain psychoanalytic or therapeutic matters accessible, to divest them of their strangeness. Like all theoretical texts, case histories principally activate the reader's cognitive abilities. The recipient's *cognitive* participation in the reading process should persuade him to accept psychoanalysis *emotionally* as both a form of philosophy and a form of therapeutic treatment. Freud worked only partially with the principles and rules of composition formulated by classical rhetoric in order to effect this kind of conviction (and therefore it is insufficient to analyse Freud's texts with critical categories derived from the study of rhetoric). Instead, he reacts to the specific problem of discourse he faced by interpolating narrative elements into his theoretical argument. Structurally speaking, his later case histories comprise five realms (or, in Freud's own words, 'fragmented portions'), which enter into multi-layered external and internal relationships. This dense network of relationships, however, is not spelled out either in form or in substance. Rather, theoretically rigorous deductions are replaced by literary structures; the reader must fill in gaps with mental images of his own and thus supply the missing connections in his endeavours to build consistency. These conjectures are thus cognitive products of the reader and not of the text, which means that they seem more plausible to the reader, and will have greater persuasive power on him than the most cogent theoretical deductions. As soon as the acceptance of a theoretical text is not based on a rational decision (a rational decision is at work whenever a theoretical notion is accepted or rejected because of the way it is presented, argued and developed), but on the fact that various textual fragments, connections, cross-connections and conclusions must be provided by the recipient, then his insight into a theoretical argument is controlled by an element that may well be described as emotional. For the reader primarily reacts to what he himself has produced, to his own mental images, and this reaction, in its turn, affects the way he feels about the text he is reading. If the recipient of the case history denies its persuasive power, he is forced to reject his own mental images or label them as inadequate, but that causes *Unlust* (unpleasure).[1] The cognitive acceptance of both the case history concerned and consequently of psychoanalysis as both a philosophy and a form of therapeutic treatment is based on the reader's attempt to avoid unpleasure. Paradoxically, then, it is by affecting his emotions that the reader's cognitive responses are brought about and, to a great extent, controlled. An extremely unusual procedure for a theoretical text!

Every case history has to integrate linear and counter-linear time axes with constellations of both a spatial and a temporal nature. In order to achieve this rather difficult task Freud, in his case history of the Wolf-Man, tells two structurally different stories, leaving the final decision as to their validity to the reader. In the first story, the beginning and end can be brought into consonance with each other, whereas the second reveals that narratives never denote but merely connote further chains of significant signs. This instance of textual self-reflexivity is a common feature of fictional texts. If it is applied to a predominantly theoretical argument, then basically two different modes of reception are possible: either the text is read (because of its self-reflexivity) as a *fictional* text, or it is read (according to its textual status) as a *theoretical* one. The second alternative is possible only if the reader, according to his own anthropological disposition, turns space and time into a meaningful whole and relates end to beginning, since these operations are not supplied by the text. His attempts to convert the openness of the text into closed gestalts results in his forcefully counteracting if not actually controlling the expansive components of the text's virtual dimension. If, however, the reader refuses to employ counteracting impulses and thus does not control the virtual dimension by divesting it of its expansiveness, then he must read the case history as a literary text. Thus no theoretical or didactic relevance will be attributed to it, and consequently its intentionality will fail – it will not carry conviction.

The virtual dimension of the literary type of psychopathography, on the other hand, is made up of different components. The communicatory situation contained in *Der Hunger nach Wahnsinn* evokes the experience of openness and expansion: the interlocking technique, the interchangeability of the individual textual fragments, the repetitions which are of great linguistic but slight semantic variability, all work towards subliminally converting the textual strategies into something which seems to be endlessly expanding. In conjunction with an imagery which connotes disgust, paralysis and anxiety, this expanding openness might topple over into a sense of oppression, especially since the openness inherent in the textual strategies is intensified even further by the expansive elements contained in the virtual dimension, that is, by the reader's individual and subjective phantasies which (because of the subject of the novel) proliferate. In *The Golden Notebook*, form (a splitting of the novel into five different perspectives), time (the systematic undermining of a time continuum) and style (a pattern of contrasting styles of writing) break open the text in such a way that the reader's active participation in processing the individual textual perspectives is required. Here, too, for the very reason that there is no interpersonally established body of knowledge about psychoses, individually based phantasies and anxieties make their way into the reading process: factors which belong to the virtual dimension of the text.

In both novels, the openness of both text and virtual dimension is countered by a specific moment of intertextuality. The literary type of psychopathography draws upon and assimilates certain patterns of representation from mediating texts. This assimilation contains an element of intentional deception, for the main and most important effect of mediating texts is stabilizing: formally speaking, they correspond – like the novel of the eighteenth century – to our ways of understanding and interpreting the world we live in, and their specific subject matter helps to balance certain deficits (especially a lack of norms). The expectation of being able to enjoy a stabilizing reading experience is brought to bear on texts dealing with psychoses. The very fact that mediating texts often stray from and even subvert the textual formula of their own genre guarantees that the intentional deception of psychopathographies will work. For if *all* mediating texts can be formally defined by five different textual aspects, then the *literary* type of mediating text is characterized by the fact that it rejects any perfect fulfilment of this paradigm and is, at least partially, innovative as well. Because the literary type of mediating text makes the reader complete missing links with his or her own mental images, these texts activate the reader's motivation for a discussion of individual reading experiences. The very fact that the literary type of mediating text, too, contains missing links, gaps and points of indeterminacy, makes it possible for psychopathographies to be read *as if they were* mediating texts. The expectation of divergent reading experiences (which is part of the literary competence the reader developed through processing mediating texts) even to some degree stabilizes the reception of texts on psychoses, at least initially. But as soon as the sense of oppression brought about by the communicatory situation of the psychopathography in question becomes so overpowering that it can no longer be stabilized and instead tips over, this sense of oppression is reinforced yet again by disappointment of the expectation of enjoying a stabilizing reading process.

The communicatory situation of those types of psychopathography which contain interesting dimensions of aesthetic response (namely, the theoretical and the literary) are thus complemented by a virtual dimension which is different for each type. Although the virtual dimension cannot be pinned down to any actual position in the text, it is still possible to describe it: it consists of expanding elements, which do not, however, implode form and structure, but are countered by other virtual factors. The counteracting forces are considerably stronger in the theoretical type than in the literary type of psychopathography; that is the very reason why the literary type – as opposed to the theoretical type – can have an oppressive effect.

To sum up: so far I have argued that all those texts belong to the literary type of psychopathography which first take psychotic attacks as their subjects, and secondly instigate a sense of oppression during the reading process. This elusive sense of anxiety is brought about by a specific interaction between the communicatory situation and the virtual dimension of the text concerned. The virtual dimension of the literary type of psychopathography is in part characterized by intertextuality, by quoting the literary formulas and the conventions of the mediating texts. However, I suspect that other literary texts – texts which do not play on this particular moment of intertextuality – may also produce effects similar to those of psychopathographies; I will confront this problem in the next chapter.

# 7

## Opening up the genre

In both types of psychopathography which give rise to interesting aesthetic responses there is an extra-textual or virtual dimension at work, consisting in part, in the literary type, of *inter*textuality. But might it also be possible for a novel to construct its virtual dimension *intra*textually? In the light of what has been discussed so far, I should expect any virtual dimension to depend to some extent on extra-textual references. Taking Doris Lessing's novel *Briefing for a Descent into Hell* (London, 1971) as an illustration, I will analyse a text which is about psychotic experience but does not draw upon the mediating texts' claim to authenticity.

Two aspects of *Briefing* strike me as unusual, one of form and one of content. The novel is divided into three levels of representation, which potentially defy integration during the reading process, and certain textual strategies impede the reader's efforts to build consistency, so that the experience of reading *Briefing* has an irritant effect, to say the least. Because of these formal criteria and their repercussions on the reader's role, *Briefing* can be described as an experiment in literary form.[1] Moreover, the novel differs from psychopathographies as I have conceptualized them so far in having one outstanding and unusual characteristic: *Briefing* is one of the very few *literary* texts relating to and interacting with a *theoretical* system,[2] namely the writings of the psychiatrist and cultural critic R.D. Laing. This specific element of intertextuality is obviously used to alleviate the problem of discourse inherent in any attempt to communicate psychosis.

Many critical studies have pointed out the influence of Laing's theory on the whole body of Lessing's fiction, and particularly on *Briefing*. Marion Vlastos, for instance, writes: 'Not only in her emphasis on madness but also in her very articulation of its value she [Lessing] shows a striking similarity to the views of R.D. Laing, unorthodox psychiatrist and cultural theoretician.'[3] Lessing herself remarked, in an interview: 'All educated people look for a key authority figure who will then act as a lawgiver. Laing became that figure.'[4] Obviously Lessing shares many of Laing's views. This may be one reason why, in the critical responses to *Briefing* – although the influence of C.G. Jung and the teachings of the Sufis on the body of Lessing's fiction are also mentioned[5] – there is a remarkable and unusual degree of agreement on the meaning of this particular text: ostensibly, the intention of *Briefing* is to illustrate one of Laing's central theses, namely that normality is madness and madness is normal. Thus, Roger Sale writes: 'The idea . . . behind *Briefing for a Descent into Hell* is easy, too easy; suffice it to say it resembles the flashy insistence of R.D. Laing that the insane are the only truly sane.'[6]

I shall not dispute the significance of Laing's theoretical system for Lessing's novel here, far from it; instead, I want to challenge the statements quoted above for not being radical enough. It is not sufficient to reduce the parallels between Lessing's novel and Laing's theory to a 'striking similarity' and the novel itself to a single idea ('the idea behind'). Moreover, most of the critical studies limit themselves to discussing the novel's substance, its plot. However, *Briefing*'s relation to Laing's theory of psychosis is not merely thematic, because certain propositions taken from Laing's theoretical system are contained in the *formal structure* of the novel, where they are juxtaposed in new and surprising ways. This montage has an alienating effect and gives rise to unexpected insights into Laing's theories.

All literary texts encapsulate parts of a 'reality beyond the text', such as certain social and historical norms and the sociocultural context in its broadest sense, and thus transcend the immanence of the text. Reality beyond the text, consisting as it does in an irritating contingency, cannot be mimetically depicted. Instead, literature usually incorporates philosophical systems in which complexity has already been reduced.[7] If literary texts, however, take over one *specific* theory in its entirety, and incorporate it not only on the thematic but also on the *formal* level, the interrelationship between literature and theory becomes very complicated indeed: different representational and communicatory techniques are required in theoretical as opposed to literary discourse. Formal devices inherent in theoretical arguments cannot simply be assimilated into literary discourse.

Where, in a literary text, a theory is drawn upon not only on the thematic level but also for the formal construction of the literary text, there are interesting repercussions on the theoretical edifice in question, which – because it has been taken over into a new, a literary context – is subject to considerable modification: certain propositions are picked up, extracted from the theory, transformed and juxtaposed in an unfamiliar way so as to give rise to unexpected and new meanings. In the specific case discussed here, it is not only the system incorporated (i.e. Laing's theory) which is modified; the encapsulation of a theoretical system also has far-reaching effects on the system which incorporates it (i.e. Lessing's novel). Moreover, the transfer of Laing's system to a literary context does not merely lead to a fundamental critique of Laing's theoretical edifice, but also – and this is one of the interesting features of *Briefing* – allows this critique to be emotionally accepted during the reading process.

For *Briefing* is not a novel which is processed purely by the intellect. On this point, I agree with Douglas Bolling, who writes: 'With some exceptions, I believe that the heavy intellectual weight of *Briefing* is expertly controlled, subordinated to narrative advance and symbolic rhythms – in short, transmuted sufficiently that the reader can respond aesthetically and emotionally rather than merely intellectually.'[8] But what are these aesthetic and emotional reactions of the reader's actually like?[9] Literary criticism has not yet produced an analysis of this novel's 'implied reader'.[10]

The formal structure, and the reader's role as contained in the text, display special features in which this novel differs from psycho-pathographies. At the same time, however, these special features allow insight into the functioning of both Laing's theory and the novel's virtual dimension. A virtual dimension is essential for communicating psychotic phenomena through literature. In *Briefing* this virtual dimension is produced and brought into play not by drawing upon the reader's literary competence, but rather by a specific narrative technique, one that is an idiosyncracy of this novel.

## R.D. Laing's anti-psychiatry

*Existential phenomenology* is the term Laing coined for his theoretical approach, which is a condensation of various very different philosophical and psychiatric traditions: he draws on both Edmund Husserl's phenomenology and Jean-Paul Sartre's existential ontology, and is indebted to Harry S. Sullivan's research into pathological interpersonal relations. One outstanding element in Laing's theory is that it lays particular emphasis on the positive and creative aspects that can potentially surface in a psychotic attack. By equating personality dissolutions with drug-induced psychedelic trips, he transforms them into a positive counterpart to our alienated everyday existence. At the same time he frees psychoses of the negativity hitherto associated with them. Laing became a cult figure of the hippie movement, where his psychiatric theories were read as conceptualizations of transcendental experience. However, his strong opposition to the negative, or at least ambivalent, assessment of personality dissolutions (which is to be found in almost all other psychiatric theories) and his denial of the high charge of anxiety they carry, lead him to ascribe much too positive a value to psychoses.

Apart from Laing's tendentious bias in his approach to his subject, however, his theory may also be criticized for inconsistency. For if one turns to his concepts looking for his definition of psychosis, its aetiology, therapy, short-term and long-term prognosis, one will find various different and contradictory statements about the same subject area. The contradictions in his argument may be attributed to the fact that Laing's theoretical approach contains four heterogeneous models of mental illness, which he draws on according to the demands of his current line of argument. These concepts – they are the conspiratorial, psychoanalytic, negative and psychedelic models [11] – do not merely exhibit contradictions regarding the theoretical basis and therapeutic indications of psychosis; they are also in part mutually exclusive. Laing himself does not expound these inconsistencies; they are merely implicitly present in his work, and can be demonstrated only by textual analyses.

Contradictions, inconsistencies and lack of precision may be fatal to the conclusiveness of a rigorous theoretical system; in Lessing's novel, however, they are the very basis for transposing theory into literature: *Briefing* destabilizes Laing's system by breaking various models of mental illness out of the very hierarchical structure upon which they rely for their function. A separate level of representation is allocated to three of the four models in the novel, and another one is present by implication. On each level, certain aspects of the protagonist's psychopathology are discussed. The three levels of representation are defined and opposed to each other through their divergent narrative perspectives. Corresponding to the absence of a hierarchical structure between the separate models as a criterion of the novel's *substance*, there is no omniscient or integrating narrative agency in the novel's *form*. The different narrative perspectives cannot be related to each other, and the various representational levels clash. Therefore, the reader's efforts to build consistency are constantly thwarted.

In Laing's theoretical edifice, on the other hand, the separate models of mental sickness are not – as in Lessing's novel – set side by side, as being of equal value, but form a hierarchic system in which the psychedelic model is dominant. In some instances (i.e. the aetiology of psychosis and the rather peculiar concept of therapy arising from it), Laing complements his psychedelic concept with a conspiratorial and a psychoanalytic factor. These factors, deriving from philosophies alien to his own theories, resist assimilation to his dominant psychedelic model. Hence the contradictions in Laing's concept. Laing manages – with considerable difficulty – to integrate the conspiratorial and psychoanalytic models into his dominant system. But he is forced to reject another model entirely, namely the negative model of mental illness. However, this model too is present in his system, even if only by implication.

The psychedelic model – a term coined not by Laing himself, but by Siegler and Osmond[12] – emphasizes the idea that psychoses consist primarily in heightening the individual perceptive capacity to an amazing extent. Such heightened sensitivity confers visionary powers upon anyone going through a psychotic episode, powers whereby he is able to surmount his alienated existence; experiencing these powers will subsequently have a positive effect on his personality profile. Laing writes: 'They [future men] will see that what we call "schizophrenia", was one of the forms in which, often through quite ordinary people, the light began to break through the cracks in our all-too-closed minds' (PE, p. 107).[13] And: 'The "ego" is the instrument for living in *this* world. If the "ego" is broken up, or destroyed (by insurmountable contradictions of certain life situations, by toxins, chemical changes, etc.), then the person may be exposed to other worlds, "real" in different ways from the more familiar territory of dreams, imagination, perception or phantasy' (PE, pp. 114f). Laing equates 'insurmountable contradictions of certain life situations' (an allusion to the 'double-bind' structures studied by Gregory Bateson)[14] with 'toxins', i.e. drugs, for according to Laing both are factors capable of inducing personality dissolutions. Laing thus attributes the aetiology of psychosis to the family structure, thereby referring to the conspiratorial model of mental sickness which I shall discuss in more detail later. To draw such undifferentiated parallels between psychedelic and psychotic states, however, is not just precariously dangerous with regard to the statement itself (which contains a naive glorification of psychoses and drug-induced states) but, moreover, it is wrong as a phenomenological description: psychedelic states are induced consciously and voluntarily, whereas psychotic states occur at random, are bewildering and charged with anxiety for the person affected. Further differences lie in the extremely different duration and the possibility, or impossibility, of voluntarily bringing one's heightened capacity of perception to an end.

Laing's phenomenological description of the psychedelic model comes to a climax with his statement:

The madness that we encounter in 'patients' is a gross travesty, a mockery, a grotesque caricature of what the natural healing of that estranged integration we call sanity might be. True sanity entails in one way or another the dissolution of the normal ego, that false self competently adjusted to our alienated social reality: the emergence of the 'inner' archetypal mediators of divine power, and through this death a rebirth, and the eventual re-establishment of a new kind of ego-functioning, the ego now being the servant of the divine, no longer its betrayer. (PE, p. 119)

The widely scattered fields of reference to which Laing's imagery relates in this quotation – they range from medicine ('natural healing') through psychology ('false self', 'ego-functioning') and sociology ('alienated social reality') to religion ('rebirth', 'the divine') – make it clear once again that his argument is situated in extremely contrary areas (some of them even tinged with metaphysics), which helps neither their internal coherence nor their ability to carry conviction.

### Doris Lessing, *Briefing for a Descent into Hell*: literature replaces theory

All these statements of Laing's about his psychedelic model of psychotic phenomena are picked up on that level of representation in Lessing's novel which thematizes a psychotic experience. Laing's model is translated into narrative technique and challenged. Lessing's protagonist, Charles Watkins, is confronted with abnormal experiences; his uninterrupted speech documents psychotic upheaval from a subjective, interior perspective. The schematic stages devised by Laing in his book *The Politics of Experience* to describe a 'journey into the unconscious' (Laing's metaphor for personality dissolutions) – that is, such a journey's form and substance – can even serve as a summary of the events depicted in Lessing's novel. Laing writes:

The person who has entered this inner realm (if only he is allowed to experience this) will find himself going, or being conducted – one cannot clearly distinguish active from passive here – on a journey. This journey is experienced as going further 'in', as going back through one's personal life, in and back and through and beyond into the experience of all mankind, of the primal man, of Adam and perhaps even further into the being of animals, vegetables and minerals. In this journey there are many occasions to lose one's way, for confusion, partial failure, even final shipwreck; many terrors, spirits, demons to be encountered, that may or may not be overcome. (PE, p. 104)

To support his ideas about the course of such an experience, Laing chiefly deploys the persuasive power inherent in life as it is experienced and, in particular, as it is narrated, quoting the 'authentic' account given by one of his patients, the sculptor Jesse Watkins. The interrelationship between Lessing's novel and Laing's theory is indicated by the similarity of the names of Laing's patient and Lessing's protagonist Charles Watkins.

Charles Watkins, too, describes a repetition of ontogenetic and phylogenetic stages of development: the ocean and dolphins, an island with flora and fauna reminiscent of ancient mythology, the climbing of a cliff, an archaic or apolcalyptic city, mythical cult sites, buildings arranged in circles and squares, and also dark influences, sinister moonlight, violent acts, murder and, finally, personified Greek and Roman gods who bring about a return to earth, *a descent into hell*.

Such a summary of content reads like a painfully exact translation of Laing's ideas into literary discourse.[15] But it does not do justice to Lessing's novel, in that the processes which occur during reading cannot be reduced to a semantic dimension. Arguing with Iser's theory of aesthetic response, this level of representation is characterized by the fact that the recipient's endeavours to build consistency – one of his most important activities during the reading process – are irritated and even thwarted.

The journey is narrated by the protatonist's inner voice. This voice is self-assured and competent in depicting the protagonist's own thoughts and feelings, and his existence in the world. The protagonist's ego structure, with its self-contained, intrapersonal voice, does not bear the least resemblance to the fragmented ego structure surfacing during psychotic experiences. Moreover the intrapersonal voice is conscious of a linear flow of time; at least, that is how the events are narrated. There are no digressions or overlapping narrative positions. In addition, the voice's linguistic competence is unobstructed. The laws of syntax and grammar are never violated. One sentence always leads logically to the next. Therefore, it is not difficult for the reader to form mental images of what he is reading. Nevertheless, the reader's attempts to build consistency out of these mental images are irritated, at least initially. This, however, is due not to a fragmentation of the narrating voice, but to a lack of contextualization. The narrative is anchored only inadequately in the context of the novel. *Briefing* begins with the observation:

> At midnight the police found Patient wandering on the Embankment near Waterloo Bridge. They took him into the station thinking he was drunk or drugged. They describe him as Rambling, Confused and Amenable. Brought him to us at 3 a.m. by ambulance. During admittance Patient attempted several times to lie down on the desk. He seemed to think it was a boat or a raft. Police are checking ports, ships, etc. Patient was well dressed but had not changed his clothes for some time. He did not seem very hungry or thirsty. He was wearing trousers and a sweater, but he had no papers or wallet or money or marks of identity. Police think he was robbed. He is an educated man. (p. 9)[16]

There follows an account of the medicaments given, and then a narrative begins without any further introduction:

I need a wind. A good strong wind. The air is stagnant. The current must be pounding along at a fair rate. Yes, but I can't feel it. Where's my compass? *That* went days ago, don't you remember? I need a wind, a good strong wind. I'll whistle for one. I would whistle for one if I had paid the piper. A wind from the East, hard on to my back, yes. Perhaps I am still too near the shore? After so many days at sea, too near the shore? But who knows, I might have drifted back again inshore. Oh no, no, I'll try rowing. The oars are gone, don't you remember, they went days ago. No, you must be nearer landfall than you think. The Cape Verde Islands were to starboard – when? Last week. Last *when*? That was no week, that was my wife. The sea is saltier here than close in shore. A salt salt sea, the brine coming flecked off the horses' jaws to mine. On my face, thick crusts of salt. I can taste it. Tears, seawater. I can taste salt from the sea. From the desert. The deserted sea. Sea horses. Dunes. The wind flicks sand from the crest of dunes, spins off the curl of waves. Sand moves and sways and masses itself into waves, but slower. Slow. The eye that would measure the pace of sand horses, as I watch the rolling gallop of sea horses would be an eye indeed. Aye Aye. I. I could catch a horse, perhaps and ride it, but for me a sea horse, no horse of sand, since my time is man-time and it is God for deserts. Some ride dolphins. Plenty have testified. I may leave my sinking raft and cling to the neck of a sea horse, all the way to Jamaica and poor Charlie's Nancy, or, if the current swings me South at last, to the coast where the white bird is waiting. (pp. 10f)

This exposition interferes with and almost impedes the reader's efforts to build consistency. Frequently, there are abrupt, unmotivated alternations between present and past tenses, although that does not seem to interrupt the chronology of the intrapersonal voice's perception. Therefore, the divergencies from a good continuation in the handling of time cannot be explained in terms of plot. The use of language, too, is an irritant. For although the macrostructure of Lessing's novel imitates and to a certain extent incorporates Laing's theories, the novel still has to face the problem of how to convey a psychotic experience – or, to be more precise, a psychedelic journey – in discourse. Contrary to what we came to expect (metaphorical language), language in *Briefing* seems to function according to the laws of the primary process; it takes on a certain similarity to the language of dreams. Symbols abound. Consequently, the tale of the journey into intrapsychic realms appears to be almost devoid of its communicative function. All three factors – a language similar to that of dreams, a lack of contextualization, and frequent, unmotivated alternation between tenses – join forces in undermining the reader's attempts to build consistency.

The psychedelic journey is translated into language by an abundance of

symbols, and every single symbol, in itself, is overdetermined. The juxtaposition of these overdetermined symbols results in complicated patterns
of interacting chains of significant signs. The symbols themselves can be
classified into four areas of origin. They arise from:

the Western cultural tradition (thus, for instance, certain constellations of
   planets recurring in the novel connote the world of the gods in ancient
   Greek and Roman mythology, which in their turn connote the world of
   Jewish, Muslim and Buddhist legend, the legends connote plots of
   modern science fiction novels etc.);
Lessing's other novels (symbols which, throughout her rather hetero-
   genenous fictional work, appear again and again, but in different
   contexts, are the sea, the ideal city – generally laid out geometrically –
   and the earthly paradise);[17]
symbolism specific to *Briefing* (this idiosyncratic symbolism is linked to
   the concepts contained in the novel's title;[18] all these concepts, too, are
   overdetermined), and,
the protagonist's unconscious (some of these symbols have an unequivo-
   cal meaning attributed to them later in the novel).

Each individual symbol is overdetermined because it not only connotes
the chains of significant signs which relate to its own area of origin, but
also, and simultaneously, refers to the chains of significant signs pointing
to other areas of origin, owing to their juxtaposition, in close proximity,
to other symbols. Thus, no symbol is ever capable of denoting meaning
and significance in any unambiguous, straightforward way. Instead,
meaning consists in potentially endless chains of free-floating
connotations.

The individual symbols, their four distinct areas of origin, and the
intricate pattern of multiple, intertwining chains of significant signs
(connoting ever more, contiguous chains of significant signs) undermine
a reading process in which the reader could decode and analyse each of
the symbols and thus produce some kind of a 'sub-text'. Such a sub-
text, substantiated by relatively unambiguous, straightforward mental
images, would be a mere figment, and an inadequate one at that, because
of the multiple overdetermination and the density of the symbolism at
work. Instead, the reader is forced to subject his interpretations, i.e. his
attempts to invest the individual symbols with meaning, to constant
modification, since the meaning of the symbols shifts.

The recipient's endeavours to build consistency may encounter irritation on the level of representation dealing with the psychedelic journey,
but they by no means fail. The negation of meaning and significance is not
all–encompassing, but partial and functional. On the one hand, it com-
municates cognitive insights into the form and function of the images

produced by the primary process, images whose substance potentially
defies denotation. On the other hand, however, it is the very density and
over-determination of the symbols introduced that open up a space within
which the reader's creativity can play around. In this realm, an unequivo-
cal decoding of the symbols is replaced by chains of free associations
stimulated by their very multiplicity. The reception process of this level of
representation, consequently, contains a strongly expansive factor: the
reader's phantasies – individual and subjective images not anchored in
the text – abound. The reader will probably perceive this playful activa-
tion of his own creative potential, instigated but not controlled by the
text, as exciting and pleasurable.

In the theoretical and the literary types of psychopathography,
proliferations of phantasies about the subject area in question are part of a
virtual dimension. In *Briefing*, on the level of representation which deals
with a psychedelic/psychotic experience, a free flow of associations is
stimulated by the very factors which also impede the building of consistency. Proliferating phantasies are thus tied to the textual strategies in
this novel, in contrast to the psychopathographies analysed above, where
they are solely linked to their subject matter.

In *Briefing*, this expansive openness is counteracted by another level of
representation, interlocking with the tale of the psychedelic/psychotic
journey and – unlike the intrapersonal voice's monologue – consisting of
dialogue: fragments of conversation are quoted, particularly the attempts
of the hospital staff to communicate verbally with the patient, attempts
which always fail. On this second level of representation, to which I shall
refer from now on as that of the hospital context, belong case notes
written by the doctors treating the patient. They use their contradictory
perception of changes in the protagonist's symptoms as the occasion for
argument about possible means of treatment. The case notes, however,
primarily document the absurdity of trying to express psychotic personality dissolutions in conventional medical terminology. Although the
doctors dealing with the case are unable to agree about what is going on,
they share a common therapeutic aim: they want to restore the patient to
'normality' by treating his manifest symptoms of insomnia, restless
activity and phantasizing with psychopharmacological drugs.

Here the second level of representation picks up another of Laing's
models of mental sickness, and a much more problematical one: Laing's
concept of mental illness as a psychedelic journey differs markedly from
classic psychiatry's understanding of psychotic phenomena, which is
scientifically objectivist in nature and sees psychosis as expressing itself
through specific symptoms, either genetically inherited or constitu-
tionally caused; the symptoms themselves remain in the last resort incomprehensible. Laing's dogged opposition to conventional psychiatry is in

itself extremely biased and undialectic; the possibly valid insights offered by somatological psychiatry can no more be integrated into his theories than can the emancipatory impact of Italian anti-psychiatry. In his theoretical writings, however, Laing does not go so far as to deny that psychopathology exists as a phenomenon, although that would be a logical deduction from his basic concept of psychosis as an intrapersonal journey. Instead, he holds that classic psychiatry is actually responsible for bringing about such psychotic phenomena,[19] as passages like the following clearly show:

> Julie, at the time I knew her, had been a patient in a ward of a mental hospital since the age of seventeen, that is, for nine years. In these years she had become a typical 'inaccessible and withdrawn' chronic schizophrenic. She was hallucinated, given to posturing, to stererotyped, bizarre, incomprehensible actions; she was mostly mute and when she did speak it was in the most 'deteriorated' 'schizophrenese'. . . . In clinical psychiatric terminology, she suffered from depersonalization; derealization; autism, nihilistic delusions; delusions of persecution, omnipotence; she had ideas of reference and end-of-the-world phantasies; auditory hallucinations; impoverishment of affects, etc. (DS, p. 178)

Thus there is a glaring contradiction in Laing's work between his concept of the 'psychedelic journey' and a concept of individual psychopathology, which exists ('she was hallucinated, given to posturing, to stereotyped, bizarre, incomprehensible actions'), but cannot be integrated into his system and must thus be split off and rejected, his negative concept.

In Lessing's novel, the psychedelic and the negative concepts are freed from the static relationship in which they are confined in Laing's theory where, as concepts one of which is dominant and one split off, they are evaluated very differently. In *Briefing*, they confront one another on neutral ground. Where Laing himself says it is his intention to show 'that there is a comprehensible transition from the sane schizoid way of being-in-the-world to a psychotic way of being-in-the-world' (DS, p. 17), this 'comprehensible transition' is omitted in Lessing's novel, and so is the hierarchy of concepts which effects the smooth transitions between them. The two levels of representation clash. Outer physical space and inner psychic space are isolated from one another. Because of the differences in narrative perspectives, and the lack of an all-encompassing narrative agency, the two levels of representation appear to resist integration. The subsuming of the negative concept of mental illness under the concept of the psychedelic journey, as proposed in Laing's theory, is rejected in Lessing's novel.

The situation as described so far, the clash between an intrapersonal perspective and an interpersonal perspective on psychotic events, might suggest that this clash should be regarded as the literary version of one of Laing's central propositions, the 'mind-body-split'. Laing writes: '[such persons] seem . . . to have come to experience themselves as primarily split into a mind and a body. Usually they feel most closely identified with the "mind" ' (DS, p. 65). In favour of such an interpretation is the fact that the intrapersonal events are presented by the voice of a lyrical I: the protagonist, while losing his sense of self during his psychotic attack, is stimulated by the associative flow of various lively images, while at the same time he dissociates himself from his own body. Against this interpretation is the fact that we have here not two dialogically organized perspectives of the protagonist's, but an interpersonal and an intrapersonal perspective, that is to say, that one of them is attributed to him by others. The clash of perspectives arises from a split between the self of the protagonist and a self as constituted for him by other people. These others do not consider the protagonist as a 'self', as a person, but only as a pathologically afflicted body. The split between these different views is further widened by the specific narrative perspective employed on the second level of representation. As opposed to the protagonist's subjective intrapersonal perspective, the narrative agency here retreats entirely behind the apparent neutrality of factual material: the norms and conventions of dramatic genres are used, utterances made by the characters are documented in the form of direct quotations, the narrative agency refrains from any evaluative comments. Because of these very different perspectives, I consider it more adequate to interpret the two divergent levels of representation in the novel as a translation into literary discourse of the two divergent concepts of mental sickness which co-exist in Laing's theory.

In contrast to the level of representation containing the psychedelic journey, which is marked by an expansive proliferation of phantasizing, no projective and complementary mental images or proliferating phantasies are possible on the level of representation which mirrors Laing's negative model. Instead, the interlocking of this level of representation with the level of the psychedelic journey effects pauses, breaks in the reader's free flow of associations. However, as the level of representation dealing with the psychiatric context occupies relatively little space, and the uncontrolled proliferation of subjectively based phantasies is only occasionally counteracted, the dominant response to reading the entire first part of the novel is that of a pleasurable production of associations, of playing with one's own creative capacities.

Somewhere around the middle of the novel, there is a break. The level containing Laing's concept of the psychedelic journey and the level dealing with his negative concept of mental illness both come to an abrupt end. The tale of psychedelic experiences in a narrative technique which presents an abundance of symbols stops, and the protagonist begins a boring life of daily routine whose effect is almost sterile: after the identity of Charles Watkins has been established, he is still suffering from amnesia, and therefore his personality profile has to be reconstructed through his relationships with other people. The protagonist, however, rejects the social roles resulting from these attempts at reconstruction. Letters from his wife, his mistress, his colleagues and other people cast various different lights on the person Charles Watkins was before his psychedelic/psychotic journey. He himself gives a written account of some of his wartime experiences which, when confronted with the other statements about his personal past, appears to be a mere phantasy product.

The second half of the novel consists entirely of this level of representation, which corresponds to yet another concept of mental illness contained in Laing's theory: since psychoses are seen to be consciousness-raising rather than psychopathological in his dominant concept (the psychedelic one), psychosis as the layman's label for a state of mind can arise only from a conspiratorial act. It is a destructive indictment, the work of the sick person's network of close social relationships, his family. Even as a medical diagnosis the imputation of 'psychosis' is unacceptable to Laing, and admission to hospital, in his view, will always assume the character of violent and unjust detention. The bias of these ideas corresponds to both his psychedelic and his negative concepts of sickness. However, Laing can fit his conspiratorial concept into his theoretical construct only by splitting off an important factor in psycho-pathology, namely suicide. In view of the great charge of anxiety in psychotic personality dissolutions, there is in fact a high risk of suicide. Although his conspiratorial concept can be integrated into the hierarchy of his theories only by neglecting large quantities of important data, it has a particular value within Laing's system, for he attributes to it the function of permitting hypotheses about the aetiology of psychotic phenomena.

In his early book *The Divided Self* (London, 1960), Laing postulates a certain logic inherent in the individual's life history as the cause of psychosis. As early as 1964, Laing was differentiating this therapeutic idea, which centres on the analysis of the individual's system of experience, in that he came to see psychotic behaviour as connected with the communicatory structures of those families in which such phenomena occur. According to Laing, these families are characterized by a rigid assignment of static roles, a repression of conflicts, and fatal double-bind situations. By implication, however, this means that Laing is restricting his phenomenology, which he calls social, to the phenomenology of the family isolated from society.

In *Briefing*, the protagonist's relationships – which appear to be rather pathological – are reconstructed in the second part of the novel. Its aesthetic effect is characterized by the fact that expectations of various kinds are thwarted: expectations that arise partly from the context of the novel as well as those that are aroused only on this new level of representation. The narrative technique of the second part of the novel consists of assimilating the strategies and devices of epistolary novels or, to be more precise, that form of the epistolary novel in which the task of narration is divided between several people. It is a device for highlighting the apparent neutrality of the documents presented. The narrative technique of the second part of *Briefing* thus corresponds to that of the level dealing with the hospital context. One of the important functions of epistolary novels with several narrating characters is to allow the reader immediate access to the thoughts and feelings of the people in the story; their subjective utterances seem not to be filtered through the mental grid of a narrator. The different character structures emerging through the specific styles of the individual letters are more important in this genre than the plot of the novel. This important function of epistolary novels, however, is absent from *Briefing*: the letters allow hardly any speculations about the personality profiles of their writers.

But they do offer several different perspectives on the protagonist's daily life, by giving a detailed account of it. This arouses the expectation that the heterogeneous bits of information will eventually form a significant and self-contained whole from which the character of Charles Watkins will emerge. Subsequently, this expectation is thwarted, owing to the specific time structure contained in this level of representation. The letters are juxtaposed, but do not correspond to any logical temporal sequence, since they are not written consecutively but at different points in time, many of them even before the protagonist's psychedelic journey. References to time such as 'today', 'this afternoon', 'ten at night', 'on Monday week' etc., create an illusion of temporal exactitude which is meaningless in view of the lack of an all-encompassing temporal frame of reference. The more these rather ordinary but mutually contradictory details that cannot be tied down to any temporal context are given, the more extensively do the fragments seem to defy integration into a whole. Many of the pieces of information, particularly those that try to explain in retrospect some of the symbols that surfaced during the protagonist's psychedelic/psychotic experience, are bound to be disappointing because of their utter simplicity: the fact that on his intrapersonal journey Charles Watkins is twice confronted with a shining crystal disc which sucks up all life around him but spares himself, for instance, can be explained by certain wartime experiences in which he twice escaped a dangerous situation and was the only survivor. And the appearance of fragments of classical mythology is suggested by his professional concern with such material – he is a professor of classics at Oxford.

The narrative technique in the whole first part of the novel aroused the expectation of a certain formal and stylistic continuity which in turn would continue to allow a pleasurable acting-out of the reader's creative potential, even if perhaps stimulated by different formal or stylistic devices. But this expectation is not fulfilled either. The majority of the letters are marked by their use of a limited vocabulary and trite rhetorical phrases. Stylistic differences between the individual letter-writers do exist, but they are rooted in the context, and not at all likely to involve the reader in the plot of the novel in so active a way as in the first part.

The negation of those expectations aroused by the conventions of the epistolary novel, an over-simple explanation of many of the mysterious symbols which initially stimulated the reader's phantasy, and stereotyped language which leaves no room for the operation of his creative capacities, all bring about an impoverishment of the communicatory situation between text and reader. That impoverishment might frustrate the reader. In the second part of the novel, moreover, there is no room for insights relating to Laing's conspiratorial concept of mental illness, to which the third level of representation corresponds. Laing is obliged to introduce this concept into his theoretical system in order to be able to explain the aetiology of psychotic phenomena. However, Lessing's novel offers no explanation of a similar nature, for if it is impossible to reconstruct from letters either the writers' characters or the recipient's personality, their respective relationships to each other are bound to remain nondescript. Certain vague statements such as, for instance, that Watkins had few friends, do not help to fill the void. He himself, it seems, found his friendships unsatisfactory. He obviously could not acknowledge his emotions. Retrospectively, in view of his psychotic experience, one can interpret the sterility and emotional coldness revealed by the way in which the protagonist dealt with his friendships as corresponding to his schizoid personal profile. Emotional sterility is not just a characteristic of his earlier social relationships; even after his psychotic phase, Charles Watkins seems unable to reorganize his psychic structures into what would be, for himself, a 'better' personality. This is the point where Lessing's novel rejects one of the fundamental claims of Laing's theory: the emancipatory power of psychedelic experience.

In the translation of Laing's theoretical construct into literary discourse, the hierarchical structure of his separate concepts is imploded first by the juxtaposition of three concepts – including the one split off in Laing's theory – as being of equal value. In addition, the explanatory power contained in Laing's conspiratorial concept of the aetiology of psychoses is rejected; so are the positive influences Laing sees as emanating from psychedelic episodes into life after a psychotic attack. Now, although *Briefing* explicitly refers to a psychiatric theory, its virtual dimension – which may seem surprising – is more closely linked to the communicatory situation between text and reader than is the case with the two types of psychopathographies analysed earlier, that is to say, the virtual dimension does not depend so much on extra-textual factors. Whereas in both the theoretical and the literary type of psychopathography, the virtual dimension consists to a large extent of the reader's individual phantasies about psychoses, in *Briefing* these phantasies are contained in and pre-structured by the narrative technique prevalent in the first part of the novel. Proliferations of expanding phantasies are triggered off by the density and multiplicity of symbols on the level of representation dealing with the psychedelic journey. Here, too, these phantasies are predominantly the reader's products; they are uncontrolled, expanding and free-floating. Therefore, they defy conceptualization.

The reader responds to the expansive openness pre-structured by the first part of *Briefing* by allowing his creative capacities to play, a basically pleasurable activity. In *Der Hunger nach Wahnsinn* and *The Golden Notebook*, however, the expansive openness pre-structured by the individual textual strategies is liable to tip over into a sense of oppression. The specific narrative technique whereby these two novels transpose a psychosis into literary discourse subliminally connotes oppression, paralysis and anxiety. Thus the reader experiences his own responses as negative, perhaps even oppressive.

The expansive openness is counteracted by two further levels of representation in *Briefing*, as opposed to *Der Hunger nach Wahnsinn* and *The Golden Notebook*, where it is countered by certain components of their respective virtual dimensions. If the counteracting forces are still relatively weak in the first half of *Briefing*, they dominate the second half of the novel to such an extent that any playful phantasizing on the part of the reader is almost completely ruled out. The reader's emotional involvement in processing the novel is likely to turn to frustration.

In *Briefing*, it is first and foremost the narrative technique (the actual textual strategies and schemata) which pre-structures the reader's involvement with the text. There are indeed rudiments of a virtual dimension in that the frustrating responses prevalent in the second part of the novel are stabilized by individual reminiscences, not contained in any actual passsages in the text, of more pleasurable reading experiences during the first part of the novel. These reminiscences give rise to the expectation that a further counter-control in the form of expansive openness will modify the dreary reading experience, but this expectation is not fulfilled. The frustration remains.

Now, the intertextual reference to Laing's theories found in *Briefing* means that it is possible to turn this frustration into a cognitive questioning of Laing's system. The reader's negative responses need not be negotiated and assimilated, but can be functionally translated into cognitive insights. Obviously, it is of the utmost importance to the dimension of aesthetic response inherent in psychopathographies – and particularly to the emotional impact they carry – that there should be a certain amount of intertextuality at work. Intertextual references should, however, be part of whatever virtual dimension is present, which means that they have to be produced by the individual reader, who subsequently feeds them into his processing of the text. If, as in *Briefing*, intertextuality is present in and tied to actual textual strategies, the reader's response will be tinged and in part controlled by a strong emotional impact, but it is highly unlikely that this emotional impact will ever tip over into a sense of oppression, as it can easily be resolved into a rational critique of Laing's concepts.

I started my analysis of *Briefing* with the question of whether other literary texts – not only those which thematize psychosis and draw on contemporary literature for their claim to authenticity – are able to instigate a sense of oppression by extrapolating emotional elements of psychotic phenomena into the reader's response. *Briefing* does this, although it is mainly the creative and positive aspects of psychoses that are communicated, while frustration is not likely to turn into a sense of oppression, but instead may lead to cognitive insights.

The second question I asked in connection with the textual analysis of Lessing's novel concerned the virtual dimension of psychopathographies. This question led to my initial conjecture that the virtual dimension of a novel always depends on intertextuality, no matter how it actually surfaces. In *Briefing*, the narrative technique necessary for relating and interconnecting literary discourse with theoretical discourse dominates the structure of the novel. Curiously, this text, unlike those analysed above, displays only rudiments of a virtual dimension. For, if intertextuality becomes part of the communicatory situation between text and reader, it is relatively easy to resolve any sense of oppression that might occur in the reader's response by turning it into a cognitive questioning of the primary text, i.e. Laing's theoretical construct. However, this cognitive questioning is emotionally conditioned and communicated, so that here we have a striking parallel between the theoretical type of psychopathography and a literary text like *Briefing*. The difference between these two texts lies in the fact that Freud's case histories control the cognitive acceptance of a theoretical edifice emotionally, whereas Lessing's novel presents an emotionally communicated critique of Laing's theory.

# 8

# Communicating psychotic phenomena through literature

While reading pathographic texts, the reader experiences some – not all – of the emotional elements inherent in psychotic personality dissolutions: pleasure and unpleasure, creative playfulness and a sense of paralysis or oppression. Three factors join forces to instigate such responses: the subject-matter of psychosis, the textual strategies and a virtual dimension which takes different forms. They are contained in actual textual strategies, and therefore can be described and analysed. Not only can one conceptualize the schemata responsible for our emotional responses to reading psychopathographies, another interesting phenomenon that the effective dimensions of all these texts have in common is the fact that there is a constant alternation between feelings experienced as positive and feelings experienced as negative. This incessant transformation is important inasmuch as is allows for a certain stabilization of the reading process: if the recipient's emotional participation in reading psychopathographies were to consist merely of unmitigated and obtrusive unpleasure, this augmentation of unpleasure would impede a good continuation of the reading process, and the reader would probably be tempted again and again to stop reading. Moreover, our aesthetic response to psychopathographies is characterized by the fact that the interchange between pleasure and unpleasure forms a distinct *pattern*. I shall now first analyse and then interpret this pattern of response. To back up my argument, I shall bring a new subject area, the psychoanalytic study of creativity, into the discussion.

Anton Ehrenzweig's psychoanalytic theory of creativity investigates in detail the way in which musicians, painters and sculptors produce works of art. Ehrenzweig is not concerned with authors, let alone with readers. None the less, his theory offers a viable way of conceptualizing the emotional dimensions contained in the reading of psychopathographies because Ehrenzweig's insights into the process of creativity suggest a parallel between the structures of creative processes which surface in the *production* of art, and those structures which enhance and limit the reading process and which are thus part of the *reception* of art. Moreover, both the production and the reception of art are characterized by a specific form of creativity, one that is, however, markedly different at each of the two poles necessary for realizing a literary work of art (author and reader). In this chapter I shall argue that the particular nature of the reading processes contained in psychopathographies can be grasped only against the background of some more general and comprehensive insights into the realms of creativity and human imagination.

In his seminal book *The Hidden Order of Art: a Study in the Psychology of Artistic Imagination* (Berkeley and Los Angeles, 1967), Ehrenzweig tries to bring order to that chaos from which the creative processes of artists spring. The origin of creativity appears chaotic because on the deepest levels of our imaginative capacities, orderly, single-stranded thinking is replaced by the multi-dimensional, disorderly and unlimited circulation of many different impulses. This 'polyphonous structure' (Ehrenzweig) arises from a superimposition of several different strands of thought upon each other. Ehrenzweig points out that artists are obviously able to alternate between rationally determined thinking and the polyphonous structure of unconscious processes, utilizing both for their purposes in new and surprising ways. Psychotics, on the other hand, are overwhelmed by the chaos of the unconscious, and subsequently lose control over their rational capacities altogether.

In order to conceptualize the hidden order of creative chaos in abstract terms, Ehrenzweig was forced to subject the 'classic' concept of an unconscious, as developed and repeatedly modified by Freud,[1] to yet another new interpretation.[2] Ehrenzweig abandoned the Freudian notion that unconscious primary processes are completely unstructured, and that primary process thinking is therefore unable to distinguish between binary oppositions. In Freud's unconscious, the concepts of time and space are non-existent, all boundaries are imploded and chaotic impulses circulate freely. In Ehrenzweig's model, on the other hand, unconscious processes are considered to be instruments of the utmost precision, which in the end prove qualitatively superior even to our rational ways of understanding the world.[3] Ehrenzweig also modifies Freud's concept of censorship,[4] that agency which separates the unconscious from the conscious: where Freud saw the *substance* of certain ideas as necessitating repression, Ehrenzweig postulates that the undifferentiated *structure* of many concepts in itself suffices to make them inaccessible to conscious thought processes. Other parts of the unconscious, however, can be utilized and exploited for ordered thinking (or, in Freudian terminology, for the secondary process).

Ehrenzweig diverges from Freud's theories on the question of how we gain access to the unconscious. According to Freud, the conscious human ego develops from the unconscious[5] by means of differentiation processes which can be only partially – if at all – undone. Only in dreams, or during psychoses, can undifferentiated impulses ever erupt from the unconscious. Ehrenzweig, however, distinguishes between two different modes of access, between *undifferentiation* and *dedifferentiation*, using undifferentiation to describe primary processes in the Freudian sense as well as certain *static* image structures which, according to Ehrenzweig, are also at work in the unconscious. Dedifferentiation, on the other hand, is that *dynamic* process which opens up the way to our unconscious resources, to our imagination and creativity.[6] Psychosis is characterized by undifferentiated chaos,[7] creativity by a structured sequence of dedifferentiating and differentiated (i.e. purposeful) modes of thinking.

The peculiarity of the dedifferentiation processes lies in the fact that our usual mode of thinking in binary oppositions is suspended, and no choice has to be made between images and thoughts which are mutually exclusive. The 'either/or' of rational thinking is replaced – and here we have a parallel to Freud's definition of the primary process – by a contingent series of images, by an 'and, and, and'. One of the fundamental problems with which creative artists are repeatedly confronted is having to make a choice between several possibilities before they have the information needed to make that choice. Unlike the secondary process, which endeavours to reduce complexity – say, by turning open into closed gestalts – dedifferentiation processes can tolerate the concurrence of the non-concurrent, the multiplicity of open forms with blurred boundaries. Ehrenzweig calls the concurrent grasping of the many different ways in which a certain problem might be solved *scanning*. Unconscious scanning is the indispensable requirement for pursuing a creative impulse in the 'right' direction.

During immersion in the realm of unconscious imagination, the weight of the images and structures characterized by static undifferentiation must not become too predominant. To prevent this, the ego must constantly oscillate between dedifferentiating and conscious thought processes. Only a reasoned train of thought can initiate such an alternation between opposed modes of perception. The ability to employ and utilize both modes of thinking simultaneously is definitely an ego function.

What psychosis and creativity have in common is a certain amount of self-destructiveness, a partial dissolution of the ego. The important difference between the two phenomena, on the other hand, is the fact that creative artists are obviously able to alternate between contrary modes of perception. Thus, from a psychoanalytic viewpoint, their egos must be extremely strong, and in this they differ from psychotics, the weakness of whose egos makes it almost impossible for them to exercise voluntary control over the alternation between opposed kinds of thinking.[8]

With the help of this construct, Ehrenzweig answered the question that had repeatedly been asked about the connections between psychosis and creativity. He did so with considerably more resourcefulness and exactitude than the humanistic theories of the nineteenth century, which merely tended to equate genius and madness.

Ehrenzweig's theoretical notions are easier to understand once one considers one of the many examples he gives. Dedifferentiation processes play a central role in all kinds of different areas; even the basic pattern of some myths and legends can be reinterpreted with the help of his model. In myth, for instance, the counterfactual movement between dedifferentiation and redifferentiation (i.e. a voluntary return to conscious thinking, to the secondary process) is substantiated. It is a part of the theme. Thus the myth of Osiris, an Egyptian fertility god, tells the tale of a fratricide: Set kills his brother Osiris and tears his body to pieces, which he scatters so as to prevent the restoration of Osiris to life. Isis, the wife and sister of Osiris, collects the scattered parts of his body, buries him, and thus enables him to live on in the earth. Here counterfactual forces, dedifferentiation and redifferentiation, are embodied in the death of being, the dissolution of physical boundaries, the scattering of the separate parts of the body, their reassembly, burial and resurrection. Countless interpretations have been given to explain the structure of this and thematically similar myths. Ehrenzweig describes them as follows:

> Rank's far-ranging material tends to cover the same ground which Frazer surveyed in his investigation of the 'dying god' theme. He too failed to account for its ubiquity. When Frazer began to collect his material, he was unable to limit it. It proliferated under his searching eyes, he had to fill volume after volume to add further to his magnum opus, *The Golden Bough*. It is said that he died a disappointed man feeling that he had not found the key to its proper understanding. One of his rationalizations was that the god-king had to die in order that a younger, more vigorous man could govern instead and ensure the fertility of the land. There is also a close connection of the theme with the invention of agriculture, perhaps the most important advance in human history. Like the dying god the seed of the corn was killed, buried in the womb of the earth, to be reborn in the spring of the new year. But one cannot interpret the vast material in either terms. The compulsion to multiply the symbolizations of the same basic theme must be rooted in a need more profound than the magic rituals of agriculture and the provision of efficient government.[9]

Ehrenzweig's own interpretation is that the theme of the dying god is a 'poemagogic' image which *symbolizes* the processes of dedifferentiation and redifferentiation and thus the basic structure of creativity.[10] Poemagogic images arise from the deepest level of the unconscious, where individuality fades and only a vague sense of being at one with the universe and all mankind still exists. (Freud called this state 'oceanic feeling'.)

What the basic structure of myths as reinterpreted by Ehrenzweig has in common with the structure of creativity is a peculiar oscillation between counterfactual movements, between expansion and contraction, or dedifferentiation and redifferentiation. In myth, this rhythm is bound to the cycle of the seasons. Corresponding to it, Ehrenzweig postulates an ego rhythm, a rhythmical movement through the various levels of our mental organization. Ehrenzweig sees this movement as essential for the functioning of *all* our mental processes, not only for the special case of creativity. It is just that the ego rhythm is more clearly marked during creative processes, and thus it can be more easily studied in the light of this phenomenon. Any perturbation within the rhythmic movement, within the oscillation between phases of 'dedifferentiation' and 'redifferentiation', results in psychopathological phenomena.[11] While functional use is made, in creative phases, of the self-destructive aspects of immersion in levels of the unconscious, in that structures showing concurrence of the non-concurrent can be subjected to unconscious *scanning*, immersion in the unconscious during psychotic attacks is almost entirely self-destructive: the ego rhythm is impeded, no dynamic movement between different modes of perception occurs, images of static undifferentiation multiply.

It is exactly this multiplication of static undifferentiation that psychopathographies attempt to translate into literary discourse. Unlike the myths analysed by Ehrenzweig, which take the motif of the dying god and use it to substantiate the dynamic movements underlying creative processes, the topic of psychopathographies is psychosis itself. They therefore challenge the flexibility of literary discourse: how can structured language convey a conglomeration of unconscious images which, according to Ehrenzweig, are inaccessible to the ego, not only because of their threatening substance but in particular because of their undifferentiated, *static structure*? Unlike creativity, psychotic phenomena are defined by the very fact that the rhythmical alternation between opposing modes of thinking is impeded.

The emotional responses to reading psychopathographies are not linear or even static, but markedly *dynamic* in structure, a phenomenon which is both curious and interesting. Phases of pleasurable reading experience alternate with oppressive phases. Only by means of such alternation can the reading of pathographical texts be stabilized at all; no reader would tolerate a reading process that induced nothing but unpleasant sensations. The reading processes contained in psychopathographies are characterized by the dynamics inherent in them, by a marked oscillation between the counterfactual forces of oppression and pleasure. Considered from the viewpoint of their oscillation between opposing modes, however, the reader's emotional responses are considerably closer to the structures of creative processes than to the chaos of psychotic undifferentiation.

The communicatory situation between text and reader in the literary type of psychopathography extrapolates 'anxiety' into the reader's response. Thus Ehrenzweig's notion of what the reception of pictorial art and music entails applies to the reception of psychopathographies too: 'Pictorial and musical space have the same capacity for compression and simultaneous expansion, stability within constant change, envelopment and repulsion. The pictorial space of great painting repels and envelops us. We may feel trapped and lost in the infinite at the same time.'[12] A sense of an enveloping oppression felt during reading, a sensation of being trapped in the text, is further enhanced by the virtual dimension of the literary type of psychopathography. This virtual dimension comprises proliferations of phantasies relating to the subject, which are expansive factors, as well as intertextual references to the conventions of the mediating texts. The dimension is *virtual* because although it is stimulated by the text, it is not contained in any definite textual strategy, and must be supplied by the reader, who may well 'feel lost in the infinite'. In the literary type of psychopathography, the intertextual references are ambivalent inasmuch as they – at least initially – counteract a strongly negative, because suspended, openness by evoking stabilizing reading experiences. The reader's expectation of stabilization, however, is thwarted, and the disappointment of his expectations reinforces his sense of an enveloping oppression to an even greater degree.

The communicatory situation pre-structured by the textual strategies of psychopathographies is expansive and open. The reader's concretization of the textual strategies is shot through by repercussions from the text's virtual dimension. This only apparently controls the expansion inherent in the text; in the last resort, the virtual dimension, too, enhances the openness of the text. Thus – at least potentially – expanding and contracting, dedifferentiating and redifferentiating forces, are at work *simultaneously*. No choice between mutually exclusive possibilities has to be made. However, that means that the textual strategies induce a reading experience which runs counter to normal perception. Ehrenzweig writes (in a different context):

Perception, particularly vision, secures our hold on reality. This is probably why we are so unwilling to accept that perception is unstable, its data shifting and subject to the interplay of the uncontrollable forces within our mind . . . perception has a different structure on different levels of mental life and varies according to the level which is stimulated at one particular time. Only in our conscious experience has it the firm and stable structure which the gestalt psychologists postulated. We have seen how, as we penetrate into deeper levels of awareness, into the dream, reveries, subliminal imagery, and the dreamlike visions of the creative state, our perception becomes more fluid and flexible. It widens its focus to comprehend the most far-flung structures. These different levels of differentiation in our perception interact constantly, not only during the massive shifts between dreaming and waking, but also in the rapid pulse of differentiation and dedifferentiation that goes on continually undetected in our daily lives.[13]

Reading about psychoses in the literary type of psychopathography opens up a way into those dimensions of experience which are situated in the deep levels of our unconscious and constantly repelled by conscious perception.

But the reader of a psychopathography can perfectly well initiate an alternation between different modes of perception during the reading process, by means of an act of will. Such a shift cannot be pinned down to any textual passage, but originates wholly with the reader. Shifts will occur only sporadically; they are essentially contingent.

As long, however, as the reader is able to tolerate the coinciding of movements running counter to each other, the concurrence of the non-concurrent, the reading of such texts opens up dimensions of experience which for the greater part remain inaccessible in real life. Reading processes offer an opportunity to experience the concurrence of mutually exclusive structures and images.

Probably no one would dispute that reading processes contain a certain amount of creativity. If we take the reading process contained in psychopathographies as a concrete example, however, receptive as opposed to productive creativity can actually be conceptualized. If productive creativity is defined as a *rhythmic* oscillation between different modes of thinking, one which has to be actively initiated by the ego functions, such an alternation will by no means be rhythmic in the reception of the literary type of psychopathography. Shifts are *contingent*. Their function is to modify unpleasure.

In order to elaborate on his notion of creativity, Ehrenzweig modified Freud's concept of the unconscious by dividing it into static and dynamic structures. Ehrenzweig's theory of creativity is defined on the one hand by an unconscious scanning of mutually exclusive phenomena, and on the other by a rhythmic oscillation between conscious and unconscious modes of perception.[14] I propose to extend his concept of creativity to include the idea that productive as well as *receptive* creativity requires toleration of the concurrence of the non-concurrent and that in both cases the ego carries out certain distinct movements. The difference between the two lies in the fact that receptive creativity does not have the rhythm essential to productive creativity.

Referred back to our example of reading about psychoses, that means that it is precisely on account of the *arhythmic* oscillation that pathological phenomena are partially conjured up by the reader. Ehrenzweig suggests that a *rhythmic* oscillation between the different forms of mental organization is part of the normal ego functions (it is merely more strongly marked in creative phases); as soon as this rhythm is interrupted, sickness or even death impend. Reading the literary type of psychopathography may be defined by a pattern of counterfactual movements which are experienced, in the recipient's emotional involvement in processing the text, as a *contingent* alternation between pleasurable and oppressive reading experiences. Mutually exclusive movements may surface simultaneously, a phenomenon which otherwise occurs in this form only in the unconscious. Whether the reader will feel this process to be enriching and pleasurable, or threatening and maybe even charged with anxiety, depends on the strength of his individual ego: on his capacity to tolerate deviant dimensions of experience.[15]

The literary type of psychopathography translates psychotic phenomena into literary discourse, although it conveys psychoses not as static undifferentiation, but as dynamic processes of dedifferentiation. During the reading of such texts, creativity (of the receptive, not of the productive kind) is mobilized and, a particularly significant point, certain emotional elements of psychoses are experienced by the reader.

In my analysis of Freud's later case histories, I showed that creative reading processes are an essential prerequisite for an adequate processing of this genre, which is didactic by intention. By the same token, our intellectual acceptance of psychoanalysis as a philosophy and as a therapeutic treatment depends on our actively investing the textual strategies with a certain amount of receptive creativity. However, in the theoretical type of psychopathography – to which case histories belong – the reader's emotional participation in reading is not controlled in the same way as in the literary type, and thus the creativity required is of a distinctly different kind too.

Case histories – like the literary type of psychopathography – face a problem of discourse. Here it is not undifferentiated, unconscious structures and images that have to be translated into literary discourse: instead, the necessity of conveying the intricacies of therapeutic technique as applied in one specific case of treatment calls on the one hand for the construction of a relation between space and time, and on the other for the integration of opposed time axes. Only if this problem of discourse is satisfactorily solved can case histories answer the basic human need for 'concord fictions' (Kermode) by opening up a route whereby the beginning and end of an occurrence may be related to each other, and thus endowing the contingency of time and human life with a 'meaning'.

In his Wolf-Man analysis, Freud takes this problem of discourse into account inasmuch as he employs specifically literary strategies. This is quite unusual in a case history, which is first and foremost didactic by intention, and is therefore steeped in the conventions of theoretical (as opposed to literary) discourse. Freud does not deduce his theoretical edifice rigorously from philosophical axioms; instead, he offers various heterogeneous perspectives on his subject area. The connections between the diverse perspectives are not part of the text, but have to be supplied by the reader. These products of the reader's do not lead into a proliferation of phantasies – as in the literary type of psychopathography – but are to a large extent controlled by their textual environment. However, if the acceptance of a theoretical text depends not upon a cognitive and rational decision, but on the fact that elements of discourse such as missing theoretical links must be supplied by the reader, reading theoretical discourse calls upon the reader's creativity to an unusual extent.

The recipient's participation in reading the Wolf-Man analysis is intensified by two further phenomena. Phantasies which are individually grounded (rather than grounded in the text) develop on account of the topic concerned, a psychoanalytic treatment. And two structurally different stories are told: Freud's discourse, in an instance of striking self-reflexivity, reveals that in one of these stories the beginning and the end can be connected, whereas the other one takes account of the poststructuralist notion that stories never denote but merely connote multiple chains of further stories. The proliferations of phantasies and the connotation of endless further stories are components of a virtual dimension. Thus, the virtual dimension of the theoretical type of psychopathography joins forces with the collapsing of space and time and of the opposing temporal axes (factors which are manifest in the text); all three press towards an expanding openness. Where in the literary type of psychopathography the virtual dimension, at least potentially, counterbalances the dynamics of the opening up of the text, in the theoretical type, the expansive impulses contained in the textual strategies and the virtual dimension are working in the same direction. The virtual dimension reinforces the tendency of the textual strategies to unmitigated expansion.

Now if the reception of this primarily didactic (and thus theoretical) text is not to founder on the fact that the text is being read as if it were literature – which would certainly entail failure to carry the intended conviction – then the reader, according to his own anthropological dispositions, must connect up space and time to make a meaningful whole and convert the dynamic openness of the text into a closed and static form. He must supply links for the heterogeneous perspectives, reduce complexity and close gestalts. The ability, indeed the desire, to convert open structures into closed gestalts is an ego function. However, that means that the reader must counter the openness of the text by throwing in the weight of his rational capacities in order to prevent it from increasing and proliferating. The counterbalancing force itself consists of a rational act of will. This conscious activity is stimulated and motivated by an impulse that is predominantly emotional, an impulse to reduce unlimited openness in order to keep the reception process from going astray.

This process will not take place in regular movements; impulses to reduce complexity and close gestalts will occur only when the openness of the text verges on a point at which it is felt to be too much of an irritant. The movements performed by the recipient in reading the theoretical type of psychopathography are marked by voluntary, *arhythmic* oscillations.

Whenever the reader sets his rational capacities to work in reading case histories, the operations of his intellectual processing of the text do not consist in logically reconstructing philosophical deductions (as might be expected, given the fact that case histories are theoretical texts), but in erratic movements dominated by defence mechanisms. Moreover, these erratic movements are stimulated by emotional factors. Dedifferentiation is counteracted by rational redifferentiation.

The formal structure of Freud's case histories contains some of the conventions of literary texts; the reading processes the case histories initiate and limit are characterized by a certain receptive creativity similar to that triggered when reading the literary type of psychopathography. The function of the case history genre, as didactic literature, cannot, however, lie in evoking a sense of oppression. Rather, such texts must be judged and evaluated according to whether they do or do not convince. Freud's case histories certainly do. However, reading his case histories calls for a considerably higher degree of receptive creativity than is usual in the reading of theoretical texts. And this is the very factor on which their power to carry conviction is founded. For if the reader were to reject the closed gestalts created by himself as untenable, wrong, meaningless etc., he would be rejecting his own products, and to do that always causes uneasiness, if not unpleasure.

Now, is it really important to invest the reading of case histories with a high degree of receptive creativity? Case histories that remain rooted in the conventions of theoretical texts, and do not employ literary methods of dealing with the problem of discourse inherent in the genre, have been examined with reference to the writings of Fromm-Reichmann. Here, the typeface itself signals the fact that theoretical considerations and the description of incidents from an actual case of psychosis therapy, i.e. two different modes of discourse, are juxtaposed. This procedure makes the reception of such case histories considerably easier, as compared with Freud's case histories; moreover, there is no virtual dimension weighing on the concretization of the textual structures. Therefore, the textual structures do not carry any impulses to expand. Processes of dedifferentiation and redifferentiation never occur. Thus, creative reading is neither necessary nor possible. Freud himself exploited the potential of the case history genre, which was his own invention, to such perfection that later case histories can only be considered degenerate forms. Innovative changes and interesting reading processes hardly occur at all in the writings of Freud's successors.

Whereas, in the theoretical type of psychopathography, creative reading proved to be an essential prerequisite for following the intention of such texts, which is to carry conviction, in Green's novel, *I Never Promised You a Rose Garden*, a literary text which does not call for any receptive creativity was examined. The lack of a virtual dimension makes it impossible to describe this novel in terms of dedifferentiation and redifferentiation. It too was classified as degenerative: as the imitative type of psychopathography.

A virtual dimension is *the essential* prerequisite for communicating certain emotional elements of psychotic phenomena in reading and for activating the reader's creativity. A virtual dimension can be effected by a wide range of different literary procedures. Intertextual references to the genre of mediating texts, which are at work in the literary type of psychopathography, are by no means a necessary prerequisite. As an example of a text which does not draw on the mediating texts' claim to authenticity, Lessing's novel *Briefing for a Descent in Hell* was analysed. Interestingly, this novel does have a strong intertextual dimension: to counteract the incommensurability of psychosis as a phenomenon of human existence with psychosis as a phenomenon of literary discourse, it interpolates certain notions taken from Laing's theoretical work. The way in which his theoretical propositions are translated into literary discourse determines the structure of the novel. Certain emotional elements inherent in psychotic processes are indeed transferred to the reader's response, but they never tip over into a sense of oppression. This is due to the fact that though the novel does open up a virtual dimension, it is considerably less marked than in the literary or in the theoretical type of psychopathography: in *Briefing*, the virtual dimension merges to a large extent with the communicatory situation between text and reader.

Proliferations of phantasy relating to the subject area may occur. However, the reader does not have to counterbalance his own phantasies himself; controlling factors are built into the text. For instance, shifts occur whenever the narrative perspective changes. Alternations between factors of dedifferentiation and redifferentiation in the reading process can generally be pinned down to actual positions in the text; they are far from being random or contingent. In the first part of the novel, the virtual dimension is almost congruent with specific positions in the text; only in the second part does it become partially detached from them. Then the reading process is stabilized by reminiscences of more pleasurable reading experiences, which give rise to the expectation that similar experiences may recur – an expectation that is thwarted again and again. On the whole, the virtual dimension is less strong and independent than in some other psychopathographies, and thus it influences the reader's emotional response in a different way. In other psychopathographies, a sense of uneasiness and unpleasure arises because the reader is reacting to something he himself has produced; in *Briefing*, any slight pangs of unpleasure that may occur can easily be attributed to definite constellations and structures in the text. This, in turn, means that the recipient is better able to deal with irritant sensations. It is conceivable that he might channel his uneasiness into a rational, critical questioning of Laing's theoretical work; after all, it is Laing's theory that is imprinted on the structural shape of this novel.

Psychopathographies – in their various different ways – pre-structure reading processes whose effective dimensions consist in an arhythmic oscillation between dedifferentiation and redifferentiation, or in the concurrence of such counterfactual forces. These forces *structurally* resemble psychotic processes, which – according to Ehrenzweig – are also characterized by arhythmic oscillations. In reading such texts, the reader does not merely experience some of the emotional elements inherent in psychosis; he even reproduces the structures of psychotic phenomena in his emotional response to the text. Reading about psychoses becomes a reading psychosis. Thus, the reading of psychopathographies allows the reader a dimension of experience in literature which remains closed to him in life.

# Glossary
# Compiled by Ernst-Peter Schneck

This glossary attempts, by elucidating some of the key concepts in this book, to bring out the reciprocal relationships between them. Its aim is to provide the reader with another instrument for understanding the text in addition to the definitions given in both the text and the notes.

### Authenticity

*See* mediating texts; narrative perspective

### Case history

Psychoanalytic case histories are of fundamental importance for the illustration, documentation and demonstration of psychoanalytic theory, although the status of case histories as theoretical discourse is ambivalent. As a kind of double historiography, the case history is faced with the necessity of integrating 'authentic' life stories, theoretical interpretations and – because linear life stories and the intricacies of therapeutic treatment run counter to each other – divergent time axes. This is made possible only by the employment of narrative strategies within a theoretical argument. In this book, the case history is conceived of as a hybrid form of text, oscillating between literary and theoretical discourse.

*See* discourse; textual strategies

### Concord fictions

Frank Kermode employs this term to characterize those fictions whose beginning and end can be related to each other, and which thus meet our fundamental need for structure and order. Such a consonance is not found only in literary plots, but also in some theoretical texts. For instance, both in psychoanalytic case histories and in psychoanalytic interpretations and therapeutic interventions, the psychoanalyst assumes a position 'at the end' and thus anchors the patient's 'history' in a closed gestalt.

*See* case history; gestalt

## Consistency-building

According to Wolfgang Iser, contoured 'places of indeterminacy' both instigate and limit a reading process, the first and foremost aim of which is to build consistency. Umberto Eco once said that our lives are as random and contingent as *Ulysses*, but we see them in terms of *The Three Musketeers*: by reducing complexity and imposing structures and order, we constantly try to convert our lives into stories as simplistic as *The Three Musketeers*. Our specific way of dealing with the contingencies of life also surfaces in our interaction with art. We attempt to transform open gestalts into closed ones, a process which the contradictions and negations in the text constantly undermine: the text will always insist on being *Ulysses*, even if we want to read it as *The Three Musketeers*.

*See* gestalt; reading; textual strategies

## Contraction

*See* dedifferentiation

## Counterfactual forces

*See* dedifferentiation

## Dedifferentiation/redifferentiation/undifferentiation/counterfactual forces

To distinguish acts of creativity from psychotic processes, Anton Ehrenzweig employs the terms 'dedifferentiation' and 'redifferentiation'. Oscillations between expanding and contracting impulses are characteristic of creativity as a dynamic process swinging between consciousness and the unconscious. The dynamics inherent in this process prevent the ego from getting stuck in a state of static undifferentiation whenever unconscious mental images surface and envelop conscious mental activity (redifferentiation is necessary to reinforce structured ways of thinking and thus to ensure mental stability). During psychotic attacks, on the other hand, the dynamic and rhythmical oscillation between consciousness and the unconscious is impeded.

*See* ego; psychosis; unconscious

## Discourse (literary v. theoretical)

The classic distinction between theoretical or referential discourse and literary or fictional discourse refers to the linguistic characteristics of the text concerned. A high degree of reduction and abstraction is typical of theoretical discourse; its intention lies in presenting an ordered and partially schematic sequence of cogent arguments. Literary discourse, on the other hand, contains contingency, subjectivity and openness. Consistency-building is our ultimate aim in reading: in theoretical texts, consistency-building is to a large extent pre-structured by the text, whereas the reader of a fictional text must do a considerable part of the structuring himself.

Today, because of the influence of modernism and postmodernism, the distinction between literary and theoretical discourse has become rather blurred. Interchanges occur: theoretical texts (for instance, case histories) employ narrative strategies, and literary texts (for instance, mediating texts) employ abstract, theoretical strategies.

*See* case history; mediating texts; modernism/postmodernism; textual strategies

## Ego

In Freud's model of the human psyche, the ego has a structuring and mediating function between the throbbing impulses emanating from the id (the unconscious) and the demands of the superego. The term 'ego' does not denote identity, but the functions and boundaries that allow identity to be established (if only tentatively). If the boundaries are weak, or if they collapse, mental images from the unconscious flood the ego (psychotic attacks).

*See* dedifferentiation; psychosis; unconscious

## Expansion

*See* dedifferentiation

## Gestalt

This term was coined by Gestalt psychology to characterize our anthropological need to form patterns and mental images out of the conflicting and essentially contingent information both life and literature offer: we constantly try to impose order by converting open gestalts into closed ones.

*See* consistency-building

## Implied reader

Wolfgang Iser's 'implied reader' is a concept that brings into view not any specific reader, but reading, the process upon which the dynamic interaction between reader and text relies. For Iser, meaning is neither pre-given nor arbitrary, but is constituted only in the act of reading. One of his basic notions is that a literary text has two poles, one artistic (created by the author) and the other aesthetic (brought into being by the reader). The two poles interact upon each other. Therefore, the 'implied reader' embraces both the formal structures in the text – its phenomenological mode of existence – and the reader's acts of consistency-building.

*See* consistency-building; gestalt; reading; reading emotions; textual strategies

### Intertextuality

A text's reference to other texts may be a matter of either form or content; a literary text may draw on literary formulas developed by other literary texts, or quote their subject matter. In psychopathographies intertextuality is a necessary prerequisite for instigating a reading process that demands the reader's active emotional participation. A curious instance of intertextuality is found in Doris Lessing's novel *Briefing for a Descent into Hell*: a theoretical edifice is transformed into literary discourse.

*See* literary competence; mediating texts; reading; virtual dimension

### Literary competence

This is a term coined by Jonathan Culler, who uses it to describe the sum of all the skills and capabilities that a reader employs, knowingly or otherwise, to process a literary text. The aesthetic effect of a text depends – according to Culler – not only on the actual strategies, schemata and perspectives it contains, but also, to a considerable degree, on the reader's ability to concretize those strategies in accordance with the knowledge he brings to the reading process.

*See* reading; textual strategies

### Mediating texts

In this book, mediating texts are classified as a genre on account of their form and not of their content. As opposed to the texts of literary modernism and postmodernism, mediating texts aim at a closely defined reading public. They evoke a certain 'authenticity' by merging divergent narrative perspectives (author, narrator and protagonist). Mediating texts have a stabilizing effect.

Over and above the characteristics that all these texts have in common, three different kinds of mediating text can be discerned:

1  In the literary type, form and content are subjected to constant modification; this type has a strongly marked drive towards innovation.
2  The theoretical type feeds on the authenticity derived from personal narrative, but employs it in the framework of theoretical discourse.
3  The imitative type merely repeats notions already well accepted by its reading public, and has no didactic or innovative value. Thus it is quickest to meet our need for a stabilizing reading experience.

Psychopathographies too fall into three textual types; their effect, however, is anything but stabilizing.

*See* discourse; modernism/postmodernism; narrative perspective; textual strategies

### Modernism/postmodernism

The texts of literary modernism and postmodernism play on the linguistic turn prevalent in modern philosophy. Modern philosophy claims that the meaning of a linguistic sign does not lie in its relation to any given object, but arises only from the various relations between linguistic signs. Therefore, language never depicts or represents meaning, but creates it.

### Narrative perspective

As an important textual strategy, the narrative perspective is crucial for structuring the reader's response to a literary text; it controls the aesthetic distance between text and reader. The first-person narrative employed in most psychopathographies, for instance, has two mutually complementary functions: it invokes a certain authenticity and at the same time decreases the aesthetic distance between text and reader.

### Personality dissolutions

*See* psychosis

### Pleasure/unpleasure

According to Sigmund Freud's 'unpleasure principle' (later re-named 'pleasure principle', see 'Beyond the Pleasure Principle', *Standard Edition*, vol. 18), human behaviour is motivated first and foremost by an attempt to avoid unpleasure, which governs all psychic activity (whether conscious or unconscious). When confronted with notions or experiences that inspire uneasiness, anxiety etc., the human being tries to substitute those for other, more pleasurable notions. For Freud, pleasure is the absence of unpleasure. Because of their destabilizing effect, psychopathographies can give rise to a sense of unpleasure in the reading process, which subsequently triggers off impulses to avoid this sensation, impulses that some psychopathographies in their turn counteract.

*See* reading emotions

### Psychosis

In psychotic attacks, the controlling and ordering mechanisms of the ego (the ego-functions and ego-boundaries) collapse. Mental images from the unconscious overwhelm and paralyse the conscious mind. The throbbing impulses from the unconscious give rise to pleasure and anxiety, to oceanic feelings and hallucinations.

*See* dedifferentiation; ego; unconscious

### Reading

Reader-oriented criticism is a lively and controversial field; it comprises a multitude of different reader constructs. All of them, however, are essentially deterministic: either the reader is dominated by the text or unlimited power over the text is ascribed to him. A way out of this dilemma is indicated by Wolfgang Iser's 'implied reader'.

*See* consistency-building; implied reader; reading emotions

### Reading emotions

Both reading intellectually and reading emotionally are grounded in language. Both forms of subjective participation in processing literature are pre-structured by strategies in the text. This book tries to conceptualize reading processes with all the conflicting factors they involve – factors which play not only on our intellect but also on our emotions – and complements Wolfgang Iser's theory of aesthetic response by psychoanalytic insights into the way we consciously and unconsciously relate to our world, insights derived from both Sigmund Freud and Anton Ehrenzweig.

*See* consistency-building; reading; textual strategies; unconscious

### Redifferentiation

*See* dedifferentiation

### Textual strategies

According to Roman Ingarden, a literary work consists of several layers, each comprising a sequence of schemata, positions, perspectives and strategies which, when processed, will 'chime in polyphonic harmony'. Iser uses Ingarden's model, but emphasizes the blanks, gaps and vacancies within each of the text's several layers; Iser highlights the immense difficulties in linking the individual schematized aspects into a harmonious whole (especially when reading modern and postmodern literature).

*See* consistency-building; implied reader; narrative perspective; reading

### Transference/counter-transference

According to Sigmund Freud, a patient in psychoanalytic treatment transfers certain psychic patterns deriving from early childhood on to his relationship with the psychoanalyst. Exploiting the patient's transference is one of the psychoanalyst's instruments for controlling the psychoanalytic treatment. As he is not only mentally but also emotionally involved in the psychoanalytic procedure, he initiates similar processes, called counter-transference. While classic psychoanalysis tries to limit counter-transference, which is viewed as unseemly and potentially harmful, the technique of corrective emotional experience, as employed, for instance, by Frieda Fromm-Reichmann, takes the opposite stance: counter-transference processes are regarded as positive, enabling and ultimately decisive for the success (or failure) of the psychotherapeutic treatment.

## Unconscious

The unconscious is not an objective entity, but a battlefield of tensions, of opposing and conflicting drives, static and dynamic image structures which can be perceived only through their effects – that is, through dreams, slips of the tongue, jokes, unconscious repetition compulsions, symptoms etc. These effects form patterns which allow for conclusions about the nature of the very conflicts upon which they are based. Moreover, psychoanalytic methods permit a conceptualization of the break between consciousness and the unconscious. Psychoanalysis thus opens up the opportunity to elaborate on the seemingly erratic and apparently irrational elements contained in the reading process, and subsequently to describe our aesthetic responses to literary texts in a more comprehensive way.

*See* psychosis; reading emotions

## Undifferentiation

*See* dedifferentiation

## Unpleasure

*See* pleasure/unpleasure

## Virtual dimension

This term – as employed in this book – denotes components beyond linguistic discourse which influence the reading process of psychopathographies. The virtual dimension can be discerned, but never pinned down to any actual position in the text. In reading the literary type of psychopathography, for instance, the reader finds that the irreconcilability of an intensively productive virtual dimension with the expectations aroused by intertextual references to mediating texts gives rise to its destabilizing effect.

*See* consistency-building; intertextuality; reading emotions

# Notes

## Chapter 1: Introduction

1 'Der ver-rückte Diskurs der Sprachlosen. Gibt es eine weibliche Ästhetik?' *Notizbuch* 2, 1980, p. 48.

2 Texts which, though they depict the emotional dimension of phenomena such as auditory and visual hallucinations, attribute them to the use of psychedelic drugs and not to psychic conflicts do not belong to the psychopathography genre: i.e. texts such as William Burroughs, *The Naked Lunch* (New York, 1959); or Carlos Castaneda, *The Teachings of Don Juan: a Yaqui Way of Knowledge* (Berkeley, 1968).

   Novels which are set in psychiatric hospitals, but are not thematically centred on a psychosis, are also excluded from the general definition. For instance, in Ken Kesey's *One Flew Over the Cuckoo's Nest* (New York, 1962), the protagonist, who is orginally mentally stable, is driven mad by the institution. Many texts which are situated in the vicinity of the psychopathography genre are polemical treatises against the institution of psychiatry. There is a long literary tradition of anti-psychiatric pamphlets. A marked increase can be traced in the publication of works on psychiatric themes in England between 1739 and 1840, corresponding to a heightened awareness of the problem in the society of that time. Running parallel to discussions of political reform, the fate of unjustly hospitalized patients in particular was at the centre of such eighteenth-century polemics, whereas in the early nineteenth century, the inhumane treatment of the mentally sick occupied that position (see Dale A. Peterson, 'Voices from the Private Madhouse in Britain (1739–1840)', *The Literature of Madness: Autobiographical Writings by Mad People and Mental Patients in England and America from 1436 to 1975*, Unpublished dissertation, University of Stanford, 1977).

3 See Karl Jaspers's definition: 'Situations commonly regarded as being felt or experienced on the borders of our existence are called . . . "borderline situations". Their common characteristic is that – in the world as divided into subject and object, the objective world – there is *nothing firm*, no indubitable absolute, nothing stable which will withstand every experience and every thought. Everything is in flow, in the constant movement of a state of being

questioned, everything, finally, is relative, split into opposites, never whole, absolute, essential' (*Psychologie der Weltanschauungen*, Berlin, 1960, p. 229).

4  See, for instance, Kurt Eissler, *Goethe. Ein psychoanalytische Studie*, 2 vols (Frankfurt, 1983 and 1985).

5  The works of David Bleich (see, for instance, his book *Subjective Criticism*, Baltimore, 1978) and Norman Holland (*The Dynamics of Literary Response*, New York, 1975) document the potentialities and in particular the limitations of literary criticism working with empirical methods. As soon as the reactions of individual readers are empirically tested, the text itself disappears from view, and the readers' personality profiles alone determine the interpretation of the text. This critical procedure soon leads into conclusions about the unconscious conflicting drives underlying individual readers' character structures. Patterns in the readers' unconscious are deduced from the way they interpret literary texts. This manner of dealing with literature not only lies outside the field of literary criticism proper, but also appears highly suspect from the psychoanalytic angle.

6  See Freud, 'The "Uncanny" ' (1919), *The Standard Edition of the Complete Psychological Works of Sigmund Freud*, James Strachey (ed.) (London, 1953–1974), vol. 17, pp. 21–52. All subsequent references to Freud are to this edition.
     In his essay on 'The "Uncanny" ', Freud examines the neurotic character structures of the hero E.T.A. Hoffmann's story 'Der Sandmann'.

7  Shoshana Felman writes: 'the relationship between "literature and psychoanalysis" . . . is usually interpreted, paradoxically enough, as implying not so much a relation of coordination as one of *subordination*, a relation in which literature is submitted to the authority, to the prestige of psychoanalysis. While literature is considered as a body of *language* – to *be interpreted* – psychoanalysis is considered as a body of *knowledge*, whose competence is called upon *to interpret*. Psychoanalysis, in other words, occupies the place of a *subject*, literature that of an *object*' 'To Open the Question', *Literature and Psychoanalysis. The Question of Reading: Otherwise*, Shoshana Felman (ed.) (Baltimore, 1982), p. 5.

8  Harold Bloom's negative verdict on psychoanalytic literary criticism is apt: 'Freudian literary criticism is like the Holy Roman Empire: not holy, not Roman, not an empire; not Freudian, not literary, not criticism', Imre Salusinszky, *Criticism in Society*, Interviews (London, 1987), p. 55.

9  See Marie Bonaparte, *Edgar Poe: Étude psychanalytique* (Paris, 1933), probably the best-known example of psychoanalytically orientated biography. By far the most impressive pathographic study is Karl Jaspers, *Strindberg und Van Gogh. Versuch einer pathographischen Analyse unter vergleichender Heranziehung von Swedenborg und Hölderlin* (Leipzig, 1922); this study is indebted to existentialist psychology (as opposed to Bonaparte's psychoanalytic approach). Pathographic interpretations of literature are not outdated methods of literary investigation, as one might think from the publication dates of the two studies mentioned above; psychopathographic studies are published even today (see, for example, Alexander Mitscherlich (ed.),

*Psycho-Pathographien: Schriftsteller und Psychoanalyse*, Frankfurt, 1972).

10 For a detailed discussion of the theoretical and methodological problems arising from any correlation of psychoanalysis or psychopathology and literature, see Bernd Urban and Winfried Kudszus, 'Kritische Überlegungen und neue Perspektiven zur psychoanalytischen und psychopathologischen Literaturinterpretation', *Psychoanalytische und psychopathologische Literaturinterpretation*, Bernd Urban and Winfried Kudszus (eds) (Darmstadt, 1981), pp. 1–13.

11 For a discussion of the role of emotions in Aristotle's theory, see W.B. Stanford, *Greek Tragedy and the Emotions: an Introductory Study* (London, 1984).

12 Since then, generations of writers and critics have returned to the question of whether responding emotionally to art is positive or negative. Evaluating the subjective elements in our involvement with art is an integral part of all aesthetic theories. The readers' emotions are usually related to the philosophical foundations of the aesthetic theory in question, and are judged within this frame of reference. Nevertheless, the highly volatile history of emotions in the history of aesthetics has yet to be written.

13 For example, W.K. Wimsatt and Monroe C. Beardsley, in their programmatic essay 'The Affective Fallacy', postulate: 'Emotion, it is true, has a well known capacity . . . to inflame cognition, and to grow upon itself in surprising proportions to gains of reason', *Twentieth Century Literary Criticism*, David Lodge (ed.) (London, 1972), p. 349.

14 Frank Lentricchia, *After the New Criticism* (Chicago, 1980), p. 18.

15 René Wellek and Austin Warren, *Theory of Literature* (New York, 1956), p. 147.

16 Northrop Frye, *Anatomy of Criticism* (Princeton, 1957), p. 4.

17 Ibid.

18 Ibid., p. 12.

19 'Metapsychology' is a term coined by Freud to describe the theoretical dimensions of psychoanalysis. In particular, the differentiation of Freud's theory into several concepts of the way the human psyche functions belongs to metapsychology. (Freud developed six such models in his work.) Metapsychology is one of the three main pillars upon which psychoanalysis rests, together with the technique of psychoanalytic treatment and the theoretical assumptions emerging from the treatment of actual cases. For a detailed discussion of this concept, see J. Laplanche and J-B. Pontalis, *The Language of Psychoanalysis* (London, 1973).

20 Nor can statements be made about the ultimate origin of the collective unconscious. As something timeless yet shared by all human beings, the collective unconscious acquires the status of an anthropological constant, something which in itself is extremely dubious.

21 Frye distances himself – at least verbally – from Jung: 'Emphasis on impersonal content has been developed by Jung and his school, where the communicability of archetypes is accounted for by a theory of a collective unconscious – an unnecessary hypothesis in literary criticism, so far as I can judge' (*Anatomy of Criticism*, pp. 111f).

However, Frye's concept owes considerably more to the Jungian model than Frye himself is willing to admit. Literary theoreticians from very different camps are entirely agreed on this point. See, for instance, Frederick Crews, a psychoanalytic literary critic: 'Token gestures of skepticism can become a means of escape from considerations of plausibility – as, for example, in Professor Frye's statement that the collective unconscious is "an unnecessary hypothesis in literary criticism" . . . even while he has been developing an immanent and impersonal notion of creativity that seems to demand that very hypothesis' (*Out of My System*, New York, 1975, pp. 72f). And the Marxist Lentricchia writes: 'Frye, we recall, eschews the help of Jungian psychology and the neo-Kantian philosophy of symbolic forms, not by denying the obvious conceptual parallels from the work of Jung and Cassirer, but by suggesting that Jung and Cassirer are unnecessary because criticism as a scientific and systematic discipline can go it alone on its own conceptual basis, since the necessary concepts are intrinsic to the discipline' (*After the New Criticism*, p. 108).

22  See the comments of Elizabeth Wright on the subject: 'For Jung the collective unconscious is the pure source of art, muddied somewhat by the "tributaries" from the personal unconscious. The more muddied it is the more it becomes a symptom rather than a symbol' (*Psychoanalytic Criticism: Theory in Practice*, London, 1984, p. 72).

23  This observation derives from the parallel between Jung and Frye. Frye himself is a formalist; he does not deal with problems of literary effect or with feelings in his *Anatomy of Criticism*.

24  Audience-oriented criticism, by centring on the *reader*, brings a long-ranging development within literary theory to an end: the nineteenth-century's obsession with the *author* as genius (Shakespeare, Dante, Goethe) gave way to Russian Formalism, Prague Structuralism and, finally, the New Criticism: critical schools interested only in the formal aspects of the *text*.

But re-orientation towards the reader is also the legacy of Aristotle's *Poetics*. Novels and poetry – as opposed to drama, to which Aristotle's aesthetics relates – are the genres upon which the textual experience of this school is based, i.e. exactly that kind of literature which Aristotle did not examine to any great extent.

25  Susan R. Suleiman writes: 'Audience-oriented criticism is not one field but many, not a single widely trodden path but a multiplicity of crisscrossing, often divergent tracks that cover a vast area of critical landscape in a pattern whose complexity dismays the brave and confounds the faint of heart' ('Introduction: Varieties of Audience-oriented Criticism', *The Reader in the Text*, Susan R. Suleiman and Inge Crossman (eds), Princeton, 1980, p. 6).

26  For a comprehensive analysis of the various reader constructs, see Wolfgang Iser, 'Readers and the Concept of the Implied Reader', *The Act of Reading: a Theory of Aesthetic Response* (Baltimore and London, 1980), pp. 27–38.

27  A further possible way of classifying the different reader constructs would be to point out their respective philosophical foundations. This method is chosen by Suleiman: 'We may distinguish, for the sake of exposition, six varieties of (or approaches to) audience-oriented criticism: rhetorical; semiotic and struc-

turalist; phenomenological; subjective and psychoanalytic; sociological and historical; and hermeneutic. These approaches are not monolithic (there is more than one kind of rhetorical or hermeneutic criticism), nor do they necessarily exclude each other' ('Introduction: Varieties of Audience-oriented Criticism', pp. 6f).

Suleiman's system of classification, too, is ultimately orientated towards the cognitive aim of the theories concerned, which in turn is determined by their respective philosophical provenance.

28 See Hans Robert Jauss, 'Literary History as a Challenge to Literary Theory', *Toward an Aesthetic of Reception* (Minneapolis, 1982).

29 Jonathan Culler argues: 'To read a text as literature is not to make one's mind a *tabula rasa* and approach it without preconceptions; one must bring to it an implicit understanding of the operations of literary discourse which tells one what to look for. Anyone lacking this knowledge . . . has not internalized the "grammar" of literature' ('Literary Competence', *Reader-Response Criticism*, Jane P. Tompkins (ed.), Baltimore, 1980, p. 102).

30 Michael Riffaterre, 'Kriterien für die Stilanalyse', *Rezeptionsästhetik*, Rainer Warning (ed.) (Munich, 1975), p. 176.

31 Ibid., p. 178.

32 Stanley Fish writes: 'But what reader? When I talk about the responses of "the reader", am I not really talking about myself, and making myself into a surrogate for all the millions of readers who are not me at all? Yes and no. Yes, in the sense that in no two of us are the responding mechanisms exactly alike. No, if one argues that because of the uniqueness of the individual, generalization about response is impossible. It is here that the method can accommodate the insights of modern linguistics, especially the idea of "linguistic competence", "the idea that it is possible to characterize a linguistic system that every speaker shares". This characterization, if it were realized, would be a "competence model", corresponding more or less to the internal mechanisms which allow us to process (understand) and produce sentences that we have never before encountered. It would be a spatial model in the sense that it would reflect a system of rules preexisting, and indeed making possible, any actual linguistic experience' (*Is There a Text in This Class?*, Cambridge, 1980, p. 44).

33 Fish admits as much, turning ironically on himself, for instance, in publishing the following anecdote: 'On the first day of the new semester a colleague at Johns Hopkins Unversity was approached by a student who, as it turned out, had just taken a course from me. She put to him what I think you would agree is a perfectly straightforward question: "Is there a text in this class?" . . . my colleague said, "Yes, it's the *Norton Anthology of Literature*," . . . "No, no," she said, "I mean in this class do we believe in poems and things, or is it just us?" Now it is possible . . . to read this anecdote as an illustration of the dangers that follow upon listening to people like me who preach the instability of the text and the unavailability of determinate meanings' (ibid., p. 305).

34 Erwin Wolff, 'Der intendierte Leser', *Poetica* 4, 1971, p. 166.

35 Norman Holland, 'Unity Identity Text Self', *Publications of the Modern Language Association* 90, 1975, p. 814.

36 Holland writes: 'As readers, each of us will bring different kinds of external

information to bear. Each will seek out the particular themes that concern him. Each will have different ways of making the text into an experience with a coherence and significance that satisfies . . . The overarching principle is: identity re-creates itself, or, to put it another way, style – in the sense of personal style – creates itself. That is, all of us, as we read, use the literary work to symbolize and finally to replicate ourselves. We work out through the text our own characteristic patterns of desire and adaptation. We interact with the work, making it part of our own psychic economy and making ourselves part of the literary work' (ibid., p. 816).

37  'In short, we put the work together at an intellectual or esthetic level as we do in terms of fantasy or defense – according to the same overarching principle: identity re-creates itself' (ibid., p. 818).

38  Rudolf E. Kuenzli reaches the same conclusion: 'Recent attempts to deal with the role of the reader (George Poulet, Umberto Eco, Michael Riffaterre, Gerald Prince, Norman Holland, David Bleich, Stanley Fish, Hans Robert Jauss, Roland Barthes, and others) have emphasized the importance of the reader for literary theory and criticism, but their speculations tend to imply two kinds of determinism: either the reader's role is determined by the text, and an ideal reader is posited; or the text is determined by the sociological and/or psychological make-up of the individual reader, and the text is reduced to an indeterminate Rorschach blot' ('The Intersubjective Structure of the Reading Process: a Communication-oriented Theory of Literature', *Diacritics* 10, 1980, pp. 47f).

39  Iser writes: 'The literary work has two poles, which we might call the artistic and the aesthetic: the artistic pole is the author's text and the aesthetic is the realization accomplished by the reader. In view of this polarity, it is clear that the work itself cannot be identical with the text or with the concretization, but must be situated somewhere between the two. It must inevitably be virtual in character, as it cannot be reduced to the reality of the text or to the subjectivity of the reader, and it is from this virtuality that it derives its dynamism. As the reader passes through the various perspectives offered by the text and relates the different views and patterns to one another he sets the work in motion, and so sets himself in motion, too.

  If the virtual position of the work is between text and reader, its actualization is clearly the result of an interaction between the two, and so exclusive concentration on either the author's techniques or the reader's psychology will tell us little about the reading process itself. This is not to deny the vital importance of each of the two poles – it is simply that if one loses sight of the relationship, one loses sight of the virtual work' (*The Act of Reading*, p. 21).

40  Roman Ingarden, *The Literary Work of Art* (Evanston, 1973); and *The Cognition of the Literary Work of Art* (Evanston, 1973).

41  See Ingarden, *The Literary Work of Art*, pp. 276ff.

42  Iser writes: 'In literary works . . . the message is transmitted in two ways, in that the reader "receives" it by composing it. There is no common code – at best one could say that a common code may arise in the course of the process. Starting with this assumption, we must search for structures that will enable

us to describe basic conditions of interaction, for only then shall we be able to gain some insight into the potential effects inherent in the work. These structures must be of a complex nature, for although they are contained in the text, they do not fulfill their function until they have affected the reader. Practically every discernible structure in fiction has this two-sidedness: it is verbal and affective. The verbal aspect guides the reaction and prevents it from being arbitrary; the affective aspect is the fulfillment of that which has been prestructured by the language of the text. Any description of the interaction between the two must therefore incorporate both the structure of effects (the text) and that of response (the reader)' (*The Act of Reading*, p. 21).

43 Bleich – like Holland – works with empirical methods. His theory is so closely related to Holland's that both critics may be placed in the same category of reader-response criticism. See also note 5 above.

44 Holland, for instance, describes the method of his book *The Dynamics of Literary Response* as follows: 'One can analyze literature objectively, but how or why the repeated images and structures shape one's subjective response – that is the question this book tries to answer. I shall have to rely rather heavily on my own responses, but I do not mean to imply that they are "correct" or canonical for others. I simply hope that if I can show how my responses are evoked, then others may be able to see how theirs are. As with most psychoanalytic research, we must work from a case history, and in this situation, the case is me. Sometimes, I am sure, my experience will coincide with yours . . . At other times, you may feel that my response is idiosyncratic – so be it' (pp. xvif).

45 Jonathan Culler, *On Deconstruction: Theory and Criticism after Structuralism* (London, 1983), p. 39.

46 See the debate between Fish and Iser in *Diacritics* 11, 1981, tellingly entitled 'Why No One's Afraid of Wolfgang Iser' (pp. 2–13) and 'Talk like Whales' (pp. 82–7).

47 In the past few years two more works on psychopathographies have been published: Thomas Anz, *Literatur der Existenz: Literarische Psychopathographie und ihre soziale Bedeutung im Frühexpressionismus* (Stuttgart, 1977); and Alexander Mitscherlich (ed.) *Psycho-Pathographien. Schriftsteller und Psychoanalyse* (Frankfurt, 1972). Both studies employ conventional pathographical methods.

48 Mediating texts are texts written in the context of the counter- or subculture of the 1960s and 1970s. Large areas of feminist literature, for instance, belong to the genre, particularly those which employ conventional literary forms and procedures.

49 The definition of psychopathographies as an intertextual reaction to the genre of mediating texts means that I shall treat them first and foremost as a *phenomenon of contemporary literature*. Therefore I shall refer only briefly here to another possible way of approaching my subject, i.e. to the question of how madness has been represented in the literature of the past.

Psychopathologies appear sporadically in many early writings, particularly the *spiritual autobiographies* of the Puritans, who endeavoured, however, to draw spiritual conclusions from daily life rather than from abnormal experiences (see G.A. Starr, *Defoe and Spiritual Autobiography*, Princeton, 1965, p. 28). If, none the less, metaphysical experiences are described in these texts, they are depicted as a struggle with mysterious and largely indefinable powers (often personified in the figure of the Devil), as was also the case in the spiritual writings of the Middle Ages. There was no conscious attempt to interpret mental disturbances, delusions, auditory and visual hallucinations and similar symptoms that are beyond rational control as the manifestation of psychic conflict until the beginning of the twentieth century, when they could be related to the popularization and progressive trivialization of Freud's work.

In expressionism, representations of madness in literature abound. There they are mainly used as counter-images to the prevailing canon of middle-class virtues such as the work ethos, self-discipline, order, a sense of duty, control of the emotions, and so on. The concern of the politically committed authors of that time was to elaborate on concepts opposed to the reality they hated: 'One [could] read the sympathetic depictions of madness in expressionism either as illusionary, regressive wish-phantasies rejecting the process of civilization (irreversible, according to Elias) and growth to adult status in it, or, where the thematic aspect of suffering is dominant, as a helpless outcry against the conditions of life within modern societies' (Thomas Anz, 'Nachwort', *Phantasien über den Wahnsinn*, Expressionistische Texte, Munich, 1980, pp. 166f).

However, studying the history of madness as a literary topic, interesting as such a study might be by and in itself, will not yield any insights into the specific dimensions of reader-response inherent in the currently popular pathographical texts. Conceptualization of the emotional responses to reading about psychoses is the aim of this book.

50  A further series of texts must be briefly mentioned here, one which seems to be situated halfway between the literary and the theoretical type of psychopathography. Like the literary type, these works make use of literary strategies that feature in mediating texts, and they take their topic from case histories (they are about one particular therapy), while they do not, like case histories, lay claim to theoretically grounded explanations.

This series of texts is closely linked to the emergence of the New Therapies in California during the 1970s (the New Therapies being in their turn only one aspect of a philosophy connected in the United States with the 'Human Potential Movement', and entailing the revival of old, particularly Far Eastern philosophies). For the New Therapies, the concept of individual psychopathology does not exist; instead, their therapeutic aim is an improvement of human capacities and talents. For this reason, they have to employ divergent, i.e. unconventional, therapeutic measures. All the New Therapies share a rejection of scientific method and of theorizing about the therapeutic context, since that might encourage the intellectualization of processes whose main aim and value lies in the emotional sphere (see Stephen A. Appelbaum, *Out in Inner Space: a Psychoanalyst Explores the New Therapies*, New York, 1979). The New Therapies share their hostility to theory with large parts of the counter-culture. But they face the dilemma that their vehement rejection of theory renders it almost impossible to distinguish among individual therapeutic strands, although they must try to offer those who are interested an insight into the different therapeutic procedures. As a result of this dilemma, we have seen the American book market flooded with accounts of 'successful' therapies in recent years.

When subjected to the categories proposed in this study, these texts *cannot* be classified, as one might at first suppose, as an intermediate form between the literary and the theoretical type of psychopathography. Although they are about psychotherapy, they do not belong to the psychopathographic genre at all, for they do not convey any phenomenon that is difficult to communicate. They describe group therapies, the interaction of individual group members and the effects of therapeutic interventions, all of them topics that are relatively easy to verbalize. With regard to their content, they thus form just another series of mediating texts; they relate to potential and actual participants in psychotherapeutic groups.

51 'Unpleasure' is a term coined by Freud. See the Glossary, p. 123.

### Chapter 2: Psychopathographies and contemporary literature: the question of intertextuality

1  This phenomenon operates, for instance, in Nabokov's novel *Ada or Ardor: a Family Chronicle*. There are two different discourses entangled in *Ada*, and they call for two different readings. Reading the first discourse is essentially an intellectual enterprise. The second discourse, however, comprises an unconscious text. The literary strategies which define this unconscious text are repetition and transference. Through metaphorical substitutions and metonymical combinations (reminiscent of Lacan's theories), a circulating desire is evoked and transferred along chains of linguistic utterances. The desire in language both instigates the reader's unconscious desire and interacts with it. Reading *Ada's* unconscious text brings about an erotic tension in the reader which mirrors and reflects the passion depicted in the text. For an exemplification of this peculiar function of literary discourse, see my article 'Desire in the Text, Desire in Reading: Nabokov's *Ada* and the Intricacies of Literary Response', *Amerikastudien/American Studies* 31, 1986, pp. 141–53.
2  Mediating texts (*Verständigungstexte*) – which will be described in this chapter – make new use of long-established literary forms. Their intentionality, however, is markedly distinct from other kinds of literature: for instance, from the literature of the 1960s, which chronologically precedes them. The literature of the sixties is characterized by its insistence on the factual: it takes up political and social material ('facts'), and it quotes fragments from other kinds of text ('newspapers, reports'), which results in formal experiments and innovations (in the area of drama, the 'documentary theatre', in poetry in the 'epigrammatic didactic poem' and in prose in the 'non-fiction novel'). As opposed to that part of the literature of the sixties, which was concerned with our sociopolitical realities, and ultimately pursued political aims, mediating texts take the exploration of the individual psyche as their topic. 'New Introspection' and 'New Subjectivity' are descriptive terms

frequently applied to the mediating texts for, by comparison with the 'New Realism' of the sixties, they appear to be apolitical in their exploration of individual experience, subjectivity and psychic conflict. Obviously, a decisive break occurred somewhere between these different literatures.

3 'Literariness' is a critical term coined by the Russian Formalists. Terry Eagleton describes their approach to literature as follows: 'The Formalists started out by seeing the literary work as a more or less arbitrary assemblage of "devices", and only later came to see these devices as interrelated elements or "functions" within a total textual system. "Devices" included sound, imagery, rhythm, syntax, metre, rhyme, narrative techniques, in fact the whole stock of formal literary elements; and what all of these elements had in common was their "estranging" or "defamiliarizing" effect. What was specific to literary language, what distinguished it from other forms of discourse, was that it "deformed" ordinary language in various ways. Under the pressure of literary devices, ordinary language was intensified, condensed, twisted, telescoped, drawn out, turned on its head. It was language "made strange"; and because of this estrangement, the everyday world was also suddenly made unfamiliar. In the routines of everyday speech, our perception of and responses to reality become stale, blunted, or, as the Formalists would say, "automatized". Literature, by forcing us into a dramatic awareness of language, refreshes . . . these habitual responses and renders objects more "perceptible". For the Formalists . . . "literariness" was a function of the *differential* relations between one sort of discourse and another; it was not an eternally given property. They were not out to define "literature" but "literariness" – special uses of language, which could be found in "literary" texts' (*Literary Theory: an Introduction*, Oxford, 1983, pp. 3ff).

4 Such a theory – which would, however, have to be relatively complex – is frequently called for. As representative of many others, I will cite Chris Weedon here: 'We need a theory which can explain how and why people oppress each other, a theory of subjectivity, of conscious and unconscious thoughts and emotions, which can account for the relationship between the individual and the social' (*Feminist Practice and Poststructuralist Theory*, Oxford, 1987, p. 3).

5 'Many feminists assume that women's experience, unmediated by further theory, is the source of true knowledge and the basis for feminist politics' (Weedon, *Feminist Practice*, p. 8).

6 In the context of the Women's Movement, yet another textual phenomenon – slogans – fulfils the same function as the deteriorated literary type of feminist texts. I therefore consider it a parallel phenomenon to the imitative type of feminist texts. Slogans communicate certain insights by catchwords. The Women's Movement invented and propagated slogans such as, 'A woman without a man is like a fish without a bicycle'; 'When God created Man, she was only practising', etc. The origin of these slogans lies in advertising; slogans are also marked by the brevity typical of jokes. The fact that the Women's Movement makes use of this particular form of discourse to create a short-term sense of identity is all the more plausible in that slogans and jokes contain an anarchic, subversive element directed against the existing order,

they stress the humorous, and they defy rational criticism. See Freud, *Jokes and their Relation to the Unconscious, Standard Edition*, vol. 8.

7 See note 6 above.
8 See note 3 above.
9 See Wolfgang Iser, *The Implied Reader: Patterns of Communication from Bunyan to Beckett* (Baltimore and London, 1975); particularly the chapters on twentieth-century literature.
10 See chapter 1, p. 9.

## Chapter 3: The literary type of psychopathography

1 See chapter 1, note 19, p. 128.
2 See Freud, 'The Unconscious', *Standard Edition*, vol. 14, pp. 159–215.
3 'Dream-work' is Freud's term for the sum of all the various processes that take place while we dream. Elizabeth Wright describes dream-work as follows: 'In *The Interpretation of Dreams* . . . Freud is interested in . . . the forms taken by the language of desire, that which he calls the "dream-work". The dream-work transforms the "latent" content of the dream, the "forbidden" dream-thoughts, into the "manifest" dream-stories – what the dreamer remembers. Latent content goes piece by piece into the dream-stories via a string of associations. It is the reverse process from that traversed by the analyst, who therefore requires the patient to retrace the chain of associations in order to decode the dream. The operations of the dream-work, its subversions and distortions, take four forms: condensation (*Verdichtung*), displacement (*Verschiebung*), considerations of representability (*Rücksicht auf Darstellbarkeit*), and secondary revision (*sekundäre Bearbeitung*)' (Wright, *Psychoanalytic Criticism*, pp. 20f).
4 Thomas S. Szasz, *The Manufacture of Madness: a Comparative Study of the Inquisition and the Mental Health Movement* (New York, 1970).
5 By far the best known of these works is Freud's monograph *Psycho-analytic Notes on an Autobiographical Account of a Case of Paranoia (Dementia Paranoides)* (1911), *Standard Edition*, vol. 12, pp. 3–82, which is based on the writings of Judge Daniel Paul Schreber, *Denkwürdigkeiten eines Nervenkranken*, 1903 (new edition Frankfurt, 1973; *Memoirs of my Nervous Illness*, London, 1955). Schreber's book subsequently acquired the status of a textbook. Again and again, international research into schizophrenia offers new interpretations of the Schreber case.
6 That psychoanalytic procedure on which the whole psychoanalytic treatment is based is called 'fundamental rule'. It entails requiring the patient to verbalize everything he thinks and feels, without consciously selecting or omitting anything, even if – in his opinion – his thoughts are unpleasant, ridiculous, uninteresting or irrelevant.
7 See chapter 3, p. 29 for an explanation of these psychoanalytic terms.
8 'Rejection of verbal communication' (*sprachliche Kommunikationsverweigerung*) is a term coined by Peter Gorsen, who writes, in connection with the subject area discussed here: 'Modes of expression which at first glance

seem to belong exclusively to the realm of psychiatric investigation . . . can break away and become the stylistic vehicle for language criticism and linguistic disclosures in art and literature. The transformation of the pathological into the aesthetic enables one to regard the utterances of sectarians, the asocial, stammerers, onomatopoets, schizophrenics or other psychopaths not as wholly negative, but to consider them from the socio-critical and political angle too, where they may then be interpreted as rejection of verbal communication' ('Literatur und Psychose. Zur Rekapitulation einer grenzüberschreitenden bürgerlichen Ästhetik', *Ästhetik und Kommunikation* 3, 1972, p. 47).

9  Cf. chapter 3, particularly pp. 28–33.

10  Franz Stanzel, *Die typischen Erzählsituationen im Roman* (Vienna, 1955), p. 163.

11  This and all subsequent page numbers refer to Maria Erlenberger, *Der Hunger nach Wahnsinn* (Reinbek, 1977).

12  See chapter 1, particularly pp. 10–12.

13  For an explanation of this term, see the Glossary, p. 120.

14  See chapter 2, pp. 21–2.

15  Harold Weinrich, 'Semantik der kühnen Metapher', *Deutsche Vierteljahresschrift für Literaturwissenschaft und Geistesgeschichte* 37, 1963, p. 335.

16  Gisela Pankow, *Gesprengte Fesseln der Psychose. Aus der Werkstatt einer Psychotherapeutin* (Munich, 1968), p. 16.

17  Ibid., p. 17.

18  Freud accounts for our heightened fear of the injury to or loss of this sensory organ by the great affective charge it carries: 'We know from psycho-analytic experience, however, that the fear of damaging or losing one's eyes is a terrible one in children. Many adults retain their apprehensiveness in this respect, and no physical injury is so much dreaded by them as an injury to the eye. We are accustomed to say, too, that we will treasure a thing as the apple of our eye' ('The "Uncanny" ', *Standard Edition*, vol. 17, p. 231).

19  Sören Kierkegaard, *The Concept of Dread*, tr. W. Lowrie (London, 1944).

20  Christian Metz, *The Imaginary Signifier: Psychoanalysis and the Cinema*, (Bloomington, 1982), p. 74.

21  Particularly during a first reading, the various perspectives on the plot cannot be arranged into a convincing pattern.

22  In the preface to *The Golden Notebook* Lessing writes: 'The book speaks through its shape.' It certainly does.

23  This and all following page numbers refer to Doris Lessing, *The Golden Notebook* (New York, 1962).

24  For the question of whether psychosis and self-confrontation can be equated, see chapter 3, p. 31.

25  John L. Carey, 'Art and Reality in *The Golden Notebook*', *Contemporary Literature* 14, 1973, p. 439.

26  Literary criticism of this novel often indicates that *The Golden Notebook* calls for an unusually intensive reading process without, however, confronting the question of how this intensity is brought about through formal structures in

the text. Judith Stitzel, for instance, describes her involvement in Lessing's text as follows: 'I find her developing readers who can attend to what they might otherwise disregard. I find her stimulating mental processes which allow us to move beyond where we are to stances less comfortable' ('Reading Doris Lessing', *College English* 40, 1979, pp. 498f).

27   This pathological pattern in relating to people first appears when, in the Yellow Notebook, i.e. in a 'literary form', she is examining the structures of her relationship with her old friend Michael (given the name Paul in the Yellow Notebook): she can tolerate negative personality traits in others as little as she can in herself. To enable herself to enter into an intense relationship, she must block out certain of Paul's characteristics; she calls them 'his negative personality' and ignores them. Consequently, she sacrifices her rational judgement and her willpower ('The world of sophisticated insight has nothing to do with her feeling for Paul', p. 209) and loses more and more of her self-integrity. She becomes unable to perceive others in their individuality; she merely uses them as screens upon which to project her own conflicts and behaviour and her fragmenting consciousness: 'He will tell a story about a patient, full of subtlety and depth, but using the language of literature and of emotion. Then he will judge the same anecdote in psychoanalytical terms, giving it a different dimension. And then, five minutes later, he will be making the most intelligent and ironical fun of the terms he has just used as yardsticks to judge the literary standards, the emotional truths' (p. 209). This statement can also be interpreted as a description of the protagonist's five notebooks with their different styles of writing, which grow out of the splintering of her life into separate realms.

28   For an explanation of this term, see the Glossary, p. 123.

29   The only group that one might possibly postulate would be a self-help group of former psychiatric patients. However, most psychiatric patients *have experienced* psychotic episodes. Thus they do not belong to the target group of psychopathographies; knowledge acquired from personal experience of psychosis would constitute an individual frame of reference that would effect reading processes radically different from those of readers who are not acquainted with such borderline states.


### Chapter 4: The theoretical type of psychopathography

1   See chapter 3, particularly pp. 31f., and chapter 4, pp. 72f.

2   See chapter 3, note 6, p. 136.

3   'From the History of an Infantile Neurosis', *Standard Edition*, vol. 17, p. 13.

4   Writing about psychoanalytic case histories, Richard Kuhns had pointed out: 'A particular characteristic of Freud's style of writing is a structure similar to that of stories. From his earliest case studies . . . Freud wrote stories, the adventures of people in mental distress and difficulty . . . We can regard Freud's writing as the invention of a new literary genre created by himself: the clinical narrative, in which the development of the action alternates with

theory, theory with character analysis, and in which characters give rise to consideration of the farther-reaching conflicts of human co-existence' ('Psychoanalytische Theorie als Kunstphilosophie', Dieter Henrich and Wolfgang Iser (eds), *Theorien der Kunst*, Frankfurt, 1982, pp. 181f).

5  For a definition of metapsychology, see chapter 1, note 19, p. 128.

6  *Standard Edition*, vol. 19, pp. 1–66.

7  For a long time, Freud's case histories seemed a perfectly straightforward genre to psychoanalysts and literary critics alike: the same status was assigned to them as to Freud's metapsychological essays. Only recently have these case histories moved into the centre of critical interest and research. Feminists and narratologists, in particular, study the case histories closely, paying them the attention they deserve.

With the publication of *In Dora's Case. Freud – Hysteria – Feminism*, Charles Bernheimer and Claire Kahane (eds) (New York, 1985), important articles on the case history of Ida Bauer, the woman to whom Freud gave the fictitious name of Dora, were collected in an anthology. Dora is the only *woman* about whose psychoanalytic treatment Freud wrote a paper, although almost all the patients he treated were women ('Fragment of an Analysis of a Case of Hysteria', *Standard Edition*, vol. 7, pp. 7–122). Anna O, another famous case, was treated by Josef Breuer, not by Freud (see *Standard Edition*, vol. 2). The four other women Freud wrote about (*Standard Edition*, vol. 2, pp. 48–181) were hypnotized, not submitted to psychoanalytic treatment.

Freud's case history of Dora is marked by a conspicuous and almost perverse misunderstanding of the particular life situation in which this patient found herself. Especially by comparison with those case histories Freud wrote about his male patients, it is striking that he adopts an alarmingly negative, almost derogatory attitude towards the patient. Freud himself admits that his psychoanalytic procedure failed in this particular psychoanalytic treatment because he did not yet have a clear conception of the function of transference. Dora broke her analysis off. The aspect of Dora's case that interests feminist criticism most is the fact that Freud here explicitly raises questions about sexual difference and the nature of femininity. These are questions which become particularly relevant to those discussions of writing by women (*écriture féminine*) initiated by the French poststructuralists. Freud always presents male sexuality as the norm, female sexuality as derivative, merely a complementary form. Consequently, Dora's attempt to break out of this male-dominated hierarchy is diagnosed by Freud as hysterical behaviour.

Feminists use Freud's case histories to demonstrate and analyse patriarchy and its mechanisms of oppression, thus turning the text into a reference to a sociocultural context existing independently of it. Narratologists, on the other hand, examine textual structures; their primary interest is in decoding the complex network of interfering strategies of which a literary text consists. The feminists and the narratologists set out with different questions in mind, and examine Freud's case histories with a view to radically different ends.

Peter Brooks is one of our most important narratologists, and the author of an interesting book about narrative procedure (*Reading for the Plot*, Oxford,

1984). It is a polemic in which he defends reading for the plot against those narratologists who subscribe too one-sidely to formalism. Brooks argues that reading for the plot is far from being the inferior and contemptible activity to which many literary critics (particularly the structuralists and poststructuralists) reduce it; instead, plot and plotting are among the most exciting if most disregarded elements of the text. He does not see plot as something static. For Brooks, plot is essentially dynamic, propelled by a 'motor' which he calls desire. Desire fulfils two kinds of functions: it drives the story forward, and it induces the reader to submit to the enticing machinations of the plot. Almost as a by-product of his argument, Brooks outlines a system of Freudian aesthetics in which he applies the psychoanalytic notion of repetition compulsion to plot structure, and expresses the relation between text and reader in terms of desire. Brooks's narratological analysis of the Wolf-Man case history is brilliant and impressive. My own thinking on the problem of the theoretical type of psychopathography has been influenced by Brooks's argument.

The aim of an analysis of Freud's case histories as examples of the theoretical type of psychopathography, in the context of this book, cannot be to make statements about the patriarchal structures that are revealed in Freud's writings, or about the dynamics of a desire that motivates and propels both plot and reader. I am concerned here, rather, with an analysis of the reader's role, which is prestructured but not determined by the text, with an analysis of the 'implied reader' (see the Glossary, p. 121) in the terminology of Iser's theory of aesthetic response. In this chapter, I shall advance the argument that the reader's role contained in the case histories resembles the reader's role in the two novels discussed in chapter 3, i.e. the literary type of psychopathography (see chapter 2, pp. 33–55).

8  *Standard Edition*, vol. 17, pp. 1–122.
9  Muriel Gardiner (ed.), *The Wolf-Man by the Wolf-Man* (New York, 1971). See also Karin Obholzer, *The Wolf-Man: Sixty Years Later. Conversations with Freud's Controversial Patient* (London, 1982). Obholzer's view of the Wolf-Man analysis is essentially negative; she argues that more than five years of analysis with Freud, comprising over a thousand psychoanalytic sessions, did not lead to any change in the Wolf-Man's neurotic personality structure.
10 See also H.P. Blum, 'The Borderline Childhood of the Wolf Man', *Journal of the American Psychoanalytic Association* 22, 1974, pp. 721–42.
11 Johannes Cremerius, 'Freud bei der Arbeit über die Schulter geschaut – Seine Technik im Spiegel von Schülern und Patienten', U. Ehebald and F-W. Eickhoff (eds), *Humanität und Technik in der Psychoanalyse. Festschrift für Gerhart Scheunert zum 75. Geburtstag* (Bern, 1981), pp. 123–58.
12 Apart from the two authors already mentioned (Hannah Green and the Wolf-Man), see also Marie Cardinal, *Les mots pour le dire* (Paris, 1975) (English edition: *The Words to Say It*, Cambridge, Mass, 1983).
13 See chapter 2, pp. 19–21.
14 'Fragment of an Analysis of a Case of Hysteria', *Standard Edition*, vol. 7, pp. 16–17.

15  See J. Breuer and S. Freud, 'Studies on Hysteria', *Standard Edition*, vol. 2, p. 269; *Studien über Hysterie*, Gesammelte Werke, Frankfurt, 1952, p. 269.

16  Ibid., pp. 48–181.

17  See note 7, pp. 139–40.

18  'Fragment of an Analysis of a Case of Hysteria', *Standard Edition*, vol. 7, p. 12.

19  As the case history of the Wolf-Man should be generally known, no summary of its individual *thematic* stages – which are only of minor relevance to the argument of my study – will be given here. The suspense and the pleasure of reading it for themselves will thus be retained for those reader who do not yet know this case history.

20  Frank Kermode, *The Sense of an Ending* (Oxford, 1966), p. 18. Kermode derives his criterion for literary value from this observation: 'All these are novels which most of us would agree (and it is by a consensus of this kind only that these matters, quite rightly, are determined) to be at least very good. They represent in varying degrees that falsification of simple expectations as to the structure of a future which constitutes peripeteia' (ibid., p. 23).

21  'From the History of an Infantile Neurosis', *Standard Edition*, vol. 7, p. 13.

22  Ibid., p. 72.

23  In the case history – and obviously in the psychoanalytic treatment too – Freud neglected to thematize and subsequently interpret the patient's transference (another subjective, expanding factor). This may be one of the reasons why Freud's treatment of the Wolf-Man is considered an ultimate failure (see notes 9 and 10).

24  Wolfgang Iser, *The Act of Reading: a Theory of Aesthetic Response* (Baltimore and London, 1980), p. 97. For a detailed discussion of the interaction between text and reader, see the chapter, 'The Structure of Theme and Horizon', ibid., pp. 96–9.

25  'Primal scene' is the psychoanalytic term for an instance in a child's early years when he observes or phantasizes his parents' sexual activities. Usually, the child interprets this scene as displaying violence and brutality on the part of the father.

26  'From the History of an Infantile Neurosis', p. 103.

27  For a definition of 'primary process', see chapter 3, p. 29.

28  See also chapter 1, p. 8.

29  See Freud, 'Analysis Terminable and Interminable', *Standard Edition*, vol. 23, pp. 209–53.

30  For a discussion of the 'de-centred subject' in the philosophy of the past two decades, see Paul Smith, *Discerning the Subject* (Minneapolis, 1988).

31  Frank Kermode, *The Sense of an Ending* (Oxford, 1966), p. 40.

32  The phrases were coined by Johannes Cremerius, 'Gibt es *zwei* psychoanalytische Techniken?', *Psyche* 33, 1979, pp. 577–99.

33  Ibid., p. 595.

34  Ibid.

35  'Clinical Significance of Intuitive Processes of the Psychoanalyst', *Journal of the American Psychoanalytical Association* 1, 1955, p. 84.

36  *Psychoanalysis and Psychotherapy: Selected Papers of Frieda Fromm-*

*Reichmann*, Dexter M. Bullard (ed.) (Chicago, 1959), pp. 182f, 190, 196f, 204, 206f and 213.

37  Ibid., p. 190.

38  Kermode, *The Sense of an Ending*, p. 39.

## Chapter 5: The imitative type of psychopathography

1  This novel was made into a film with the same title by New World Pictures in 1977.

2  See chapter 4, p. 59.

3  Fromm-Reichmann writes: 'One exuberant young patient . . . was warned against expecting life to become a garden of roses after her recovery. Treatment, she was told, should make her capable of handling the vicissitudes of life which were bound to occur, as well as to enjoy the garden of roses which life would offer her at other times. When we reviewed her treatment history after her recovery, she volunteered that this statement had helped her a great deal', *Psychoanalysis and Psychotherapy: Selected Papers of Frieda Fromm-Reichmann*, Dexter M. Bullard (ed.) (Chicago, 1959), p. 204.

4  This eerie counter-reality is described by Fromm-Reichmann as follows: 'The patient had [been] . . . living for eleven years in an imaginary kingdom which she populated by people of her own making and by the spiritual representations of others whom she actually knew. They all shared a language, literature, and religion of her own creation' (ibid., pp. 206f).

5  In my research on these two texts I came across only one other reference to the striking identity of both treatments. It appears in Dale A. Peterson, *The Literature of Madness* (unpublished dissertation, University of Stanford, 1977). Peterson writes that Greenberg herself told him the novel was based on a therapy she had undergone with Fromm-Reichmann. Peterson does not go any further; he does not analyse the narrative techniques and aesthetic effects of the two texts.

6  For my discussion of this conventional literary device, see chapter 3, pp. 42f.

7  Hannah Green, *I Never Promised You a Rose Garden* (London, 1967, reprint), p. 20.

8  This phenomenon, for instance, is at the centre of a whole network of literary devices for conveying self-confrontation and psychosis in *The Golden Notebook*. See my analysis in chapter 3, pp. 42–54.

## Chapter 6: The virtual dimension of psychopathographies

1  According to Freud, the attempt to avoid *Unlust* (unpleasure) is one of the central motives of all human actions. For a definition of this term, see the Glossary, p. 123.

## Chapter 7: Opening up the genre

1  Such experiments are quite unusual in Lessing's novels. The only one besides *Briefing* to experiment with literary form is *The Golden Notebook* (see my analysis chapter 3, pp. 42–54). Most of Lessing's work is indebted to the realistic tradition of the nineteenth century. Her five-volume cycle *Children of Violence* is generally considered to be a *Bildungsroman*, a genre prevalent in the eighteenth and nineteenth centuries which today has lost almost all its force. And her cycle *Canopus in Argus* may be described, because of its subject matter, as fantasy or Utopian literature, though formally speaking it falls back on the trite and rather schematic narrative conventions of science fiction.

2  Another example of intertextuality between literature and theory is the relationship between Laurence Sterne's *Tristram Shandy* and John Locke's *An Essay Concerning Human Understanding*. An analysis of this particular instance of intertextuality is to be found in Rainer Warning, *Illusion und Wirklichkeit in Tristram Shandy und Jacques le Fataliste*, Theorie und Geschichte der Literatur und der schönen Künste, Texte und Abhandlungen 4 (Munich, 1965), pp. 60ff; also in Wolfgang Iser, *Laurence Sterne's 'Tristram Shandy'*, Inszenierte Subjektivität (Munich, 1987).

3  Marion Vlastos, 'Doris Lessing and R.D. Laing: Psychopolitics and Prophecy', *Publications of the Modern Language Association* 91, 1976, p. 246.

4  Quoted in Nancy S. Hardin, 'Doris Lessing and the Sufi Way', *Contemporary Literature* 14, 1973, pp. 571f.

5  Hardin, 'Doris Lessing and the Sufi Way'; see also Hardin, 'The Sufi Teaching Story and Doris Lessing', *Twentieth Century Literature* 23, 1977, pp. 314–26.

6  Roger Sale, *The New York Review of Books*, 6 May 1971, p. 15.

7  See Wolfgang Iser, 'The Referential System of the Repertoire', *The Act of Reading: a Theory of Aesthetic Response* (Baltimore and London, 1980) pp. 68–85.

8  Douglas Bolling, 'Structure and Theme in *Briefing for a Descent into Hell*', *Doris Lessing Critical Studies*, A. Pratt and L.S. Dembo (eds) (Madison, 1974), p. 136.

9  Bolling examines the mutual relationship of theme and symbolic structure in this novel. Guido Kums's study, with the promising title 'Structuring the Reader's Response: *Briefing for a Descent into Hell*' does indeed highlight the role of the reader, but Kums's statements are not only apodictic, they are also confined to a description of our intellectual interactions with the text: 'The main purpose of Doris Lessing's *Briefing for a Descent into Hell* is to make the reader accept a paradox: he must be brought to see his way of living in society, in his familiar world, as an abnormal mode of existence, as a crippling form of alienation – and he must be prepared to accept the visions of madness and hallucination as profound wisdom', *Dutch Quarterly Review of Anglo-American Letters* 11, 1981, p. 197.

10  'Implied reader' is a term coined by Wolfgang Iser. See the Glossary, p. 121.

11 See Miriam Siegler, Humphrey Osmond and Harriet Mann, 'Laing's Models of Madness', *British Journal of Psychiatry* 115, 1969, pp. 947–58.

12 Miriam Siegler and Humphrey Osmond, *Models of Madness, Models of Medicine* (New York and London, 1974), particularly 'The Psychedelic Model', pp. 58–65.

13 Here, and in all the following quotations from Laing, PE refers to *The Politics of Experience* (Harmondsworth, 1967) and DS to *The Divided Self* (Harmondsworth, 1965).

14 Gregory Bateson, *Mind and Nature: A Necessary Unity* (New York, 1979).

15 A critical comparison of the two narratives strictly from the viewpoint of content has already been made. See Roberta Rubenstein, 'Briefing on Inner Space: Doris Lessing and R.D. Laing', *Psychoanalytic Review* 63, 1976, pp. 83–93; Marion Vlastos, 'Doris Lessing and R.D. Laing', p. 256; Lois A. Marchino, 'The Search for Self in the Novels of Doris Lessing', *Studies in the Novel* 4, 1972, p. 259.

16 This and all following page references refer to Doris Lessing, *Briefing for a Descent into Hell* (London, 1971).

17 See Patrick Parrinder, 'Descents into Hell: the Later Novels of Doris Lessing', *Critical Quarterly* 22, 1980, p. 6.

18 See Rotraud Spiegel, *Doris Lessing: The Problem of Alienation and the Form of the Novel*, Frankfurt/Berne/Cirencester 1980, pp. 107f.

19 Laing identifies Emil Kraepelin, and that trend in psychiatric research which derives from him, as the ultimate cause for these images of mental illness. However, the concept of illness as represented by Laing exists neither in the work of Kraepelin himself nor in that of his pupils. Thus, Uwe H. Peters, in his essay 'Laings Negativmodell des Irreseins', shows 'that in the passage used to illustrate this concept Laing fiddled with Kraepelin's text and used for his interpretation precisely those passages which had been most changed' *Nervenarzt* 48, 1977, p. 478.

### Chapter 8: Communicating psychotic phenomena through literature

1 For a description of Freud's concept of the unconscious which basically entails a distinction between 'primary process' and 'secondary process' thinking, see chapter 3, pp. 28–30.

2 It seems to be characteristic of all innovations in the field of psychoanalytic research that each of them sets out from a fundamentally new concept of the unconscious. See also my discussion of Jung's 'collective unconscious', chapter 4, p. 68.

3 Ehrenzweig writes: 'We could reverse the usual evaluation and consider analytic vision cruder and less sensitive than . . . undifferentiated modes of vision obtaining on primitive . . . levels of awareness' (*The Hidden Order of Art*, p. 9).

4 See chapter 3, p. 29.

5 Cf. chapter 4, p. 68.

6 Ehrenzweig says: 'I will speak of *undifferentiation* when referring to the static

structure of unconscious image making, of *de*differentiation when describing the dynamic process by which the ego scatters' (*The Hidden Order of Art*, p. 19).

7  'In schizophrenia the unconscious fear of dedifferentiation oversteps a critical limit. The creative ego rhythm swinging between differentiated and undifferentiated levels is halted altogether. Under such extreme conditions a breakthrough of undifferentiated phantasy brings about the catastrophic chaos which we are wont to associate with the primary process' (ibid., p. 24).

8  Ehrenzweig writes: 'In mental illness undifferentiated material rises from the unconscious merely to disrupt the more narrowly focused modes of conscious discursive thinking; and the chaos and destruction which we are wont to associate with undifferentiated primary process phantasy overwhelm the patient's reason. In contrast to illness, creative work succeeds in coordinating the results of unconscious undifferentiation and conscious differentiation and so reveals the hidden order in the unconscious' (ibid., pp. 4f).

9  Ibid., p. 174.

10  'The self-destructive imagery of the "dying god" . . . did not so much symbolize masochistic phantasy as the process of creating itself, that is to say the self-destructive attack of unconscious functions on the rational surface sensibilities. These tragic images are not symbolic in the usual way; they do not express archaic or infantile drives (id), but events within the creative personality (ego)' (ibid., p. xiii).

11  'The ego could not function at all without its rhythm oscillating between its different levels . . . Impeding the rhythm spells insanity and even physical death' (ibid., p. 177).

12  Ibid., p. 94.

13  Ibid., p. 87.

14  In addition, Ehrenzweig distinguishes between three phases of creative activity, which he expresses in psychoanalytic terms. That division is not relevant in the context of this study; I will therefore mention it only briefly here. Ehrenzweig writes: 'The creative process can thus be divided into three stages: an initial ("schizoid") stage of projecting fragmented parts of the self into the work; unacknowledged split-off elements will then easily appear accidental, fragmented, unwanted and persecutory. The second ("manic") phase initiates unconscious scanning that integrates art's substructure, but may not necessarily heal the fragments of the surface gestalt . . . In the third stage of re-introjection part of the work's hidden substructure is taken back into the artist's ego on a higher mental level. Because the undifferentiated substructure necessarily appears chaotic to conscious analysis, the third stage too is beset with often severe anxiety. But if all goes well, anxiety is no longer persecutory (paranoid–schizoid) as it was in the first stage of fragmented projection. It tends to be depressive, mixed with a sober acceptance of imperfection and hope for future integration . . . Because of the manic quality of the second stage, the following "depressive" stage is all the more difficult to bear. Who has not experienced the grey feeling of the "morning after" when having to face the work done on the day before? Suddenly the ignored gaps and fragmentation and the apparent chaos of undifferentiation push into

consciousness. Part of the creative capacity is the strength to resist an almost anal disgust that would make us sweep the whole mess into the wastepaper basket' (ibid., pp. 102f).

15 Feelings arising as a result of processing literary strategies can be conceptualized only as movements which form patterns, but as each individual will react to a different degree, no statements about their intensity can be made.

# Index

subculture, literature of 19–23, 33, 132, 133
*Subjective Criticism* (Bleich) 127
'Sufi Teaching Story and Doris Lessing, The' (Hardin) 143
suicide and psychosis 102
Suleiman, Susan R. 129, 129–30
Sullivan, Harry S. 92
'symbolic order' (Lacan) 40
symbols
  in *Briefing for a Descent into Hell* 97–102, 103–4, 105
  in Jung 8, 129
symptoms 125
  in *Briefing for a Descent into Hell* 96–9
  in *The Golden Notebook* 46–52
  in *Der Hunger nach Wahnsinn* 35–42
  in *I Never Promised You a Rosegarden* 81
  of neurosis, in psychoanalytic treatment 60–70
  of psychosis 31, 38, 39, 41, 51, 74–6
synaesthesia 39
Szasz, Thomas 30

*Teachings of Don Juan, The* (Castaneda) 126
*Technik* (Morgenthaler) 71
temporal dimension
  in psychoanalytic treatment 57–74
  in reading 11–13, 43, 48, 65–6
tenses, use of, as textual perspective
  in *Briefing for a Descent into Hell* 96–7, 103
  in case histories 64–74
  in feminist literature 22
  in *The Golden Notebook* 48–9, 88
  in *Der Hunger nach Wahnsinn* 34–8
  in *I Never Promised You a Rosegarden* 82
theoretical type of
  feminist literature 25–6
  mediating text 14, 20, 26–7, 58, 122
  psychopathography 15, 33, 56–79,

80, 81, 85–9, 105, 114–17, 134, 140; *see also* case histories, psychoanalytic
  virtual dimension of 86–7, 115
theory becomes literature 16, 90–106
*Theory of Literature* (Wellek and Warren) 7
therapy *see* psychoanalytic treatment; psychosis, therapy of
topics, history of, in literature 4–5, 133
transference 33, 139, 141
  definition of 124
  in psychotherapy 32, 56, 59, 72–4
  as textual strategy 134
  *see also* counter-transference
treatment *see* psychoanalytic treatment; psychosis, therapy of
*Tribute to Freud* (H. D.) 59
*Tristram Shandy* (Sterne) 143
*typischen Erzählsituationen im Roman, Die* (Stanzel) 137
typology, literary (Frye) 7–8

' "Uncanny", The' (Freud) 127, 137
unconscious, the 12–13, 60–74, 108–9
  of author 3
  'collective' (Jung) 8, 68–9, 128–9
  communicated by reading psychopathographies 2, 34, 113–18
  and creativity 68, 108–9, 113–14, 120
  definition of 125
  desire *see* desire, unconscious
  drives pertinent to *see* drives
  Ehrenzweig's concept of 108–14, 120, 145
  Freud's concept of 29, 60–2, 68–9, 108–9, 144
  genesis of 8, 109
  Lacan's concept of 17–19, 134
  in language 18, 134
  of protagonist 3, 98
  of psychoanalyst 71, 73
  and psychosis 2, 29–33, 34, 56, 121, 123
  of reader 3, 127
'Unconscious, The' (Freud) 136